Hit Me!

Richard Carman • Jamie Gledhill • Malcolm Graham • Nicola Groag
Francesca James • Alexia Leachman • Andy Lopata • Filip Matous
Andrew Rayner • Alan Stevens • Nichola Stott • David White

As a buyer of the printed book of *Hit Me!*, you can download the full eBook free of charge. Simply point your smartphone or tablet camera at this QR code or go to: **ebooks.harriman-house.com/hitme**

Hit Me!

How to get your small business to punch its weight online

Fresh business thinking.com   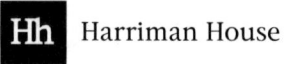 Harriman House

HARRIMAN HOUSE LTD

3A Penns Road
Petersfield
Hampshire
GU32 2EW
GREAT BRITAIN

Tel: +44 (0)1730 233870
Fax: +44 (0)1730 233880
Email: enquiries@harriman-house.com
Website: www.harriman-house.com

First published in Great Britain in 2012.

Copyright © Harriman House Ltd.

The right of the contributors to be identified as the Authors has been asserted in accordance with the Copyright, Design and Patents Act 1988.

Original chapter text remains copyright © of individual authors, 2012, all rights reserved.

ISBN: 9780857192714

British Library Cataloguing in Publication Data
A CIP catalogue record for this book can be obtained from the British Library.

All rights reserved; no part of this publication may be reproduced, stored in a retrieval system, or transmitted in any form or by any means, electronic, mechanical, photocopying, recording, or otherwise without the prior written permission of the Publisher. This book may not be lent, resold, hired out or otherwise disposed of by way of trade in any form of binding or cover other than that in which it is published, without the prior written consent of the Publisher.

No responsibility for loss occasioned to any person or corporate body acting or refraining to act as a result of reading material in this book can be accepted by the Publisher, by the Authors, by the employers of the Authors, or by Fresh Business Thinking.

Set in Baskerville and Myriad Pro.

Printed and bound in the UK by CPI Group (UK) Ltd, Croydon, CR0 4YY.

Contents

INTRODUCTION: Taming the Wild Wild Web — 1
   About Fresh Business Thinking — 2

1. SETTING UP AN ONLINE BUSINESS by Nicola Groag — 3
   About Nicola Groag — 4
   Introduction — 5
   1. The Admin Stuff — 6
   2. The Website Stuff — 8
   3. Customer Service — 12
   4. Marketing — 13
   5. Social Media — 14
   6. And Finally . . . — 14

2. HOW TO WRITE CONTENT THAT PEOPLE WILL LOVE by Alan Stevens — 15
   About Alan Stevens — 16
   Why Blog? — 18
   What Should I Put in My Blog? — 19
   What About Look and Feel? — 21
   Do I Have to Write My Blog Myself? — 21
   Can I Make Money from My Blog? — 22
   8 General Blogging Tips — 22
   15 Ways to Make Your Content More Shareable — 23

3. EMAIL MARKETING by Jamie Gledhill — 27
   About Jamie Gledhill — 28
   Why Email? — 29
   Aims and Expectations — 30
   Email Data — 35
   The Email Design — 37
   Getting Your Email Delivered — 40
   Next Step — 43

4. MARKETING WITH YOUTUBE by Filip Matous — 45
   About Filip Matous — 46
   Objective #1: Increase Reputation Within a Niche — 48

Objective #2: Humanise Your Company	53
Three Other Online Video Ideas	55
Technical Points About Video	56

5. LINKEDIN FOR REFERRALS by Andy Lopata — 61

About Andy Lopata	62
The Power of Networks	64
A Referrals Strategy	66
Being Social	68
Effective Use of LinkedIn	68
LinkedIn as a Referral Tool	70
Bypassing the Gatekeeper	71
Saving Time and Generating Results	74

6. TWITTER FOR BUSINESS by Francesca James — 75

About Francesca James	76
So How *Exactly* Can Twitter Help Your Business?	78
1. Big is Not Always Beautiful	81
2. Don't Buy Followers	82
3. Stop and Listen	83
4. Connect with Hashtags	85
5. Be Trendy with Hashtags	87
6. Bad News: Deal With It	88
7. Live Event Tweeting	89
8. Timing is Everything	90
9. Empower Your Ambassadors	90
10. Create Opportunities for Media Exposure	91
Final Thoughts	91

7. FACEBOOK MARKETING FOR SMALL BUSINESS by Nichola Stott — 93

About Nichola Stott	94
Setting Up a Facebook Page	96
How Does Facebook Marketing Work for Business?	105
Your Facebook Marketing Strategy	108
A Note on Facebook Ads and Sponsored Stories	114
Get Started!	114

8. WINNING CUSTOMERS WITH REPORTS by David White — 115

About David White	116
1. Make it Optional	118

2. Help Them First	119
3. Multiply to Identify	119
4. Keep it Real	120
5. Use Different Media	120
6. The Call to Action (I)	121
7. The Call to Action (II)	121
Final Thoughts	122

9. THE ART OF WEB DESIGN by Malcolm Graham   123

About Malcolm Graham	124
Key Metrics	127
Getting Good Scores	128
Search Engine Optimisation	130
The Basics	131
30 Worst Website Crimes	132

10. THE ART OF USER EXPERIENCE DESIGN by Richard Carman   135

About Richard Carman	136
What is UX Design?	137
The Key Elements of UX Design	139
UX Design Concepts and Best Practice	145
The Commercial Case for UX Design	147

11. ONLINE REPUTATION by Alexia Leachman   151

About Alexia Leachman	152
Reputation is What You Make it	154
It's All About the 'About'	158
Your Digital Identity	160
What Are You Doing?	161

12. LOCAL INTERNET MARKETING by Andrew Rayner   165

About Andrew Rayner	166
How Does Local Internet Marketing Work?	167
Local Search Marketing – The Basics	170
Research Your Local Search Battlefield	172
Don't Just Appear in Search, Dominate It!	174
Local Internet Marketing Doesn't Stop	175

"When I took office, only high energy physicists had ever heard of what is called the World Wide Web... Now even my cat has its own page."

– Bill Clinton

Introduction:
Taming the Wild Wild Web

BACK IN 2005, the same year that YouTube was launched, I started working on a website for entrepreneurs: **www.freshbusinessthinking.com**. Within a year, Google acquired YouTube for $1.65 billion. I haven't yet earned money of that magnitude, but I have acquired a wealth of knowledge along the way.

This book is a way of sharing that knowledge in the same way that I learnt my online lessons – from lots of different people!

One of the first things I realised was that no one knows everything about the internet and online communications – and even if for one miraculous moment they did, before they could get to their Twitter account something would have changed.

My journey involved many meetings where I asked stupid questions, bought lots of cups of coffee and made lots of new friends.

Now I'm a very well-connected 'generalist' and this book will introduce you to the specialists who understand, write and speak about their areas of expertise.

The internet and in particular social media sites have helped topple governments, made politicians more accountable and embarrassed big corporations. 33% of people in the world today are internet users. So if you own or run a business it is critical that you keep yourself informed.

The following chapters will certainly help.

Nick James
2012

About Fresh Business Thinking

Fresh Business Thinking is a resource for business owners, directors and entrepreneurs. It is where information-hungry and time-poor business decision-makers can source knowledge and advice to help them run their businesses more effectively and efficiently.

Running a business can be a lonely existence – you need to wear many hats and keep up to date with the latest developments and thinking.

The pace of business is continuously accelerating and **www.freshbusinessthinking.com** is where you can find the information you need to help drive your business forward.

SETTING UP AN ONLINE BUSINESS

by Nicola Groag

About Nicola Groag

NICOLA GROAG is a former City girl and current entrepreneur. She is the founder and CEO of luxury e-commerce boutique **www.lacoquette.com**, selling designer sex toys and luxury bedroom products, specialising in high-end online retail with an emphasis on health, luxury and discretion.

Whilst she works in e-commerce and is immersed in digital and tech, she still maintains that she is 80% creative and only 20% geek.

Introduction

IN THE MOVIE *Field of Dreams*, Ray Kinsella (played by Kevin Costner) hears a voice telling him to build a baseball diamond in the cornfields of Iowa:

"If you build it, he will come..."

Well, if I could give all you aspiring e-commerce entrepreneurs out there one piece of advice it would be this: when it comes to setting up an online business (or just building an effective website for your offline business) it is *not* as simple as 'build it and they will come'.

We all know how the internet has revolutionised shopping and e-commerce has changed the way we sell. I am not here to blind you with stats. I am here to give you some honest advice on setting up an online business, as someone who has been there and done it in a tough and niche market.

I specialise in luxury adult retail. My website sells luxury and designer sex toys and bedroom accessories. Yes, it usually is a conversation stopper. Yes, it is a challenging market. So if I can give you any pointers that will make your journey a little easier then my work here will be done.

1. The Admin Stuff

Admin may be boring, but it needs to be done: these things are the foundation of your business. Get them right first, because you are unlikely to have time to go back and fix them later.

Choose a domain name (your web address)

You want to choose your website name, check its availability as a domain and then register it.

Ah yes, it sounds so simple. It won't be. Pretty much every domain name you might want is probably already taken. Look at variations but be aware you want to have a clear, compact, memorable domain name that works easily through word of mouth as well as fitting your brand and keywords people will search for when looking for your site. Hyphens or numbers in your web address? These things will deter people. How easily would you remember web addresses with hyphens in if you were searching on Google?

Always get the .com and the .co.uk if you can. Utilise auction sites and domain registration searches (e.g. **www.sedo.com** or **uk.godaddy.com**) to see if the domain name you want can be obtained via auction purchase or direct contact with the current owner. Lots of people buy domains not to develop them but simply to hold and wait for someone like you to buy. The auction process can take a while but can be worth it if you get that distinctive URL you so desire.

Remember that for a purely online business your domain is your shop window, your brand identifier. Protect it at all costs. It is one of the most valuable assets you have. People will tell you horror stories of losing their domain names and everything they have worked for through the sheer carelessness of forgetting to renew it. Register it with a reputable internet domain registrar and then lock it down.

Register your company name

This doesn't have to be the same as your brand name or website address. For my business, for example, discretion is key – people don't want the website name splashed all over their credit card statements. So I have a very simple limited company name. You may also wish to consider registering a dormant company in the same name as your brand, in order to protect it from other people.

Protect your intellectual property

Register any logos and trademarks with the Intellectual Property Office. If you have a distinctive logo and/or brand name the last thing you want is someone copying it and selling similar products. Registering your IP will give you some protection from infringement down the line. In the UK trademark registration costs from £170 plus £50 for each additional 'class' in which you wish to register. Check out **www.ipo.gov.uk** for more detailed information.

Hosting

Hosting is vitally important for an online business. A web-hosting company will provide you with space on a server and internet connectivity for your site. The key things you need to be aware of are reliability and speed. Go for a trusted provider with the fastest web server. If your site goes down you lose money. If your customers can't connect fast enough and go elsewhere – guess what? Yes, you lose money. Don't risk it.

Budget

Budget is not a subject I am generally in any position to preach about. The harsh reality is that when you start a new business you don't have a lot of money. You can run an online business from a laptop in your spare room – many hugely successful e-commerce entrepreneurs started just like that. You don't need an office and the trappings of a corporate lifestyle. To quote Brad Burton, motivational speaker, founder of 4N Networking and author of *Get Off Your Arse* (GOYA):

> *"You don't need swivel chairs or a fish tank"*

This is true. Your money is better spent on inventory that you can turn over for a profit than office fittings that simply depreciate. However, don't make the mistake of sitting on loads of stock you can't shift – negotiate with your suppliers. Spend the money you do have wisely – a great looking, easy-to-use, optimised website; marketing that provides a return on investment (ROI) – these are your true assets.

2. The Website Stuff

Design, build and development

Wow, where to start with this? To be brutally honest, one of the key things about being in business is knowing (and admitting) your limitations. Your ego is not your amigo. Learn, absorb, try and do as much as you can do (well) yourself, but never assume you know everything. Get experts in where you need to. I am no website developer. Code might as well be in, well, code for all I know about it. It's all Geek to me.

If you can't do this well yourself, get someone to do it for you. Get a web designer who will understand your vision and help you implement it. Get a web developer who you can communicate with easily and who can operate within your budget. If these are the same person, all the better!

Choose an e-commerce software platform that is appropriate to the size and scale of your business. I chose Magento because the PHP platform provided the back-end features I wanted, and two years ago the e-commerce platform market was a lot less crowded. Now you can find numerous SaaS (Software as a Service) platforms such as Shopify, which provide a quicker, lower cost route to market but won't provide the sophisticated functionality or scalability of larger platforms. It is horses for courses and budget plays a key role here. Do the usual thing – obtain quotes, don't immediately go for the first option, be clear in your requirements and protect your vision with non-disclosure agreements (NDAs).

Ensure your website is intuitively designed for the user. You want to sell from the moment someone arrives at your site so provide a 'roadmap' that makes it easy for the customer to navigate to the next step. Call-to-action buttons (orange is the best colour for these, according to most recent research), one-step-payment pages and a secure trusted payment provider who process quickly are all vital. Remember, every step is a point at which you could lose a customer and a sale. Don't let them go! Test your site as much as you can before you go live – you don't want to end up with virtual egg on your face. But remember you can spend months testing and tweaking (and not making any money). At some point you have to just launch it and learn from anything that happens after that point.

Your website is your route to market. Make it absolutely the best it can be from a design perspective. A visual treat. Functionality is king, but aesthetics are key. You never get a second chance to make a first impression. This applies as much to virtual interaction as physical interaction. Would you go back to a shop if you couldn't find what you wanted quickly, easily and in a nice environment? Competition on the internet is tough – set yourself apart in a good way.

In the hallowed words of a true guru, Steve Jobs:

> *"Be a yardstick of quality. Some people aren't used to an environment where excellence is expected."*

In my business there are many sites out there that all look the same – functional, brightly coloured, quite frankly a bit intimidating. Let's face it, typing 'sex toys' into Google is a terrifying thought for most people. My vision for **www.lacoquette.com** was to create a boutique shopping experience on the internet. I wanted to try and recreate the luxury, aspirational shopping experience I desired when shopping for any high-end retail goods, in a market where that was not the norm. Yes, it would have been easier to go with the crowd – but that wasn't my brand vision. I did have to compromise on certain things to turn vision into function, and you might have to as well; but never be something you are not – you just won't be able to sustain it.

You have to believe in your brand vision from day one so you can communicate it to others. Your website is your brand's shop window to millions and millions of people. So, no pressure!

Search engine optimisation (SEO)

Search engine optimisation is the process of improving the visibility of your website in a search engine's natural/unpaid/organic (whatever you like to call it) search results. In general, the higher a site is ranked on the search results page, and the more frequently a site appears in the search results list, the more visitors it will receive from the search engine's users.

When I first set up my website I made a rookie error. I didn't really understand the importance of SEO and my finance director wouldn't budget for it. As a result, the website went live without being optimised for search engines.

Remember my first paragraph: 'build it and they will come'? Yeah – exactly. They didn't.

So after six months of struggling with extremely slow organic growth, throwing wasted money at print advertising while not ranking on Google searches and generally struggling to get noticed, we bit the bullet and paid for SEO.

Again, I would say get an expert to do this for you, and as they do it make sure you learn as much as you can about how to maximise your site yourself going forward. **Lacoquette.com** now ranks extremely well organically for many key words. But SEO is a constantly evolving process. Don't lose six months of customers by not building SEO into your budget from the beginning. And don't get complacent after six months of effective SEO by assuming there's nothing more you can do.

Google Analytics/AdWords

As an e-commerce entrepreneur, Google is in many ways like your dream date. Your aim is to get as close as possible to being hand in hand with Google. Learn everything you can about this powerful search engine and its associated products.

Google Analytics or GA (**www.google.com/analytics**) is a free service offered by Google that provides detailed stats about the visitors to your website. GA can track visitors from all direct and referred traffic sources, including all search engines, display advertising, pay-per-click (PPC/CPC) networks, email marketing, social media etc. You can use this to monitor your traffic, see which marketing activities are driving traffic spikes, identify areas you might want to spend more money or time marketing, and learn about your true customer demographics.

It also provides detailed information about e-commerce conversions – sales activities, keywords used and routes to transaction completion. All of this can help with your customer targeting and provide guidance on how to make your site more customer-friendly going forward. But a word of warning – don't get overly caught up spending all your time in GA. It provides a wealth of information. The important thing is knowing what to concentrate on for your business.

Google AdWords (**adwords.google.co.uk**) is Google's main advertising product (and one of its main sources of revenue). AdWords offers pay-per-click (PPC) advertising, cost-per-thousand (CPM) advertising, and site-targeted advertising for text, banner, and rich-media ads. These are the adverts you see in the coloured boxes at the top of each Google results page as well as down each side of the page. In this box, on page one, is where you want your site's ads to appear. I don't have enough words here to sum up the complexity of the Google AdWords auction process, how to set up campaigns or the importance of long tail or negative keywords. However, I would absolutely emphasise the importance of AdWords as a tool for any online business getting to new customers. When done well the value in conversions should, of course, exceed the cost. Research it, learn it, apply it. Or get someone appropriately qualified to set up your campaigns for you.

3. Customer Service

One of the key things to remember about your website is that it is *all* about the end user. Tony Hsieh, CEO of **Zappos.com** (an American online shoe retailer) wrote an amazing book called *Delivering Happiness: A Path to Profits, Passion and Purpose* all about serving the customer. Buy it, read it, absorb and learn.

The thing to remember here is that online businesses don't have a bricks-and-mortar shop – no one can come in and 'kick your tyres' or test that you aren't some fraudster taking their money and not sending them their goods. Your customers take a leap of faith to order from you. As with any relationship, you don't mess with someone's trust. In my business my customers have many trust issues to get past when ordering from me – will the products arrive discreetly as promised, will they arrive in the time frame stated, will they look like the picture on the site? I take that extremely seriously.

Customer loyalty is key, so concentrate on high levels of customer service. Develop a reputation for delivering on what you promise. Walk your talk. If you say you are going to despatch same day then do it. If problems arise – fix them fast and at your customer's convenience.

You can't buy the customer loyalty you achieve by exceeding people's expectations first time.

4. Marketing

Assuming you have covered the basics – business plan, marketing plan, unique selling point (USP) identification, demographic research, etc. – it's time to think about marketing.

At the end of the day, all of your marketing plans will be subject to change on an increasingly regular basis – view them as organic documents. Evolve, adapt, change and grow. What you write down on day one might not be appropriate on day 361 – but it's good to have some basic benchmarks.

You may not get the target market you expect. If that happens, adapt. Don't stick rigidly to your plan.

Your marketing is all about forging an online presence and reputation. Your existing customers are your best customers, so encourage their return through loyalty programmes. Then it's all about marketing to drive new traffic and new customers. When you start out, you don't have a massive marketing budget so be savvy. Spend money on AdWords where you can but focus on organic marketing growth too – it takes longer but it is worth the effort.

In the words of Gary Vaynerchuk, entrepreneur extraordinaire and author of one of my favourite business books, *Crush It! Why Now is the Time to Cash In on Your Passion*:

> *"The best marketing strategy ever? CARE"*

5. Social Media

Social media is a good marketing tool not least because, in the main, it is free. Twitter (**www.twitter.com**), Facebook (**www.facebook.com**), Pinterest (**www.pinterest.com**) and Tumblr (**www.tumblr.com**) are all worth checking out. Sign up and get to know each one.

Blog. Create a presence. Make your content relevant and valuable to your potential customers. Don't use social media to sell, sell, sell but as an additional way to create a brand that people can identify with and trust. Use social media to connect with brand influencers and potential ambassadors in your sphere. Build connections with them, particularly on LinkedIn (**www.linkedin.com**). It can be a great way to find true partners and collaborators. Social media shouldn't be like a one-night stand, but an ongoing relationship. It takes time and effort. Work on it. Make time for it when you can.

6. And Finally...

So my last pieces of advice if you are setting up an online business? Be patient – don't expect to see results overnight. Just keep going. You will make mistakes – but acknowledge them, learn from them and then move on.

And finally – be brave. You will have moments of overwhelming fear, fear of the unknown, of whether you are doing the right thing. In those moments I use as my motto the words of American entrepreneur Jim Rohn:

> *"If you are not willing to risk the unusual, you will have to settle for the ordinary."*

Never settle for the ordinary – create something fabulous.

HOW TO WRITE CONTENT THAT PEOPLE WILL LOVE

by Alan Stevens

About Alan Stevens

ALAN STEVENS is an expert on building and protecting your reputation. He is Past President of the Global Speakers Federation and director of MediaCoach.co.uk. He is also a speaker, author and journalist, and has been both a TV presenter and expert interviewee. In April 2012, he was named number 66 in the 'Top social media experts to follow on Twitter' by influential blogger and commentator Evan Carmichael.

His clients include MPs, TV presenters and sports stars as well as companies including Virgin, BP, The Dorchester, Sony Ericsson, BMW and Mumm Champagne. *The Independent* newspaper listed him as "one of the top 10 media experts in the UK".

His latest book is *The Exceptional Speaker*, co-authored with Paul du Toit. Alan may be booked to speak at your event via his site **www.mediacoach.co.uk**.

NOT EVERYONE sees themselves as a writer. Many of us believe that we either have nothing interesting to say, or that we couldn't express it well enough to engage readers. I view both beliefs as wrong. We all have something valuable to say, and we all have ways to express ourselves that will make others listen. If you still disagree, I hope that by the end of this chapter, I will have made you change your mind.

Writing online copy (a website, a blog, a Facebook post or an article) is a process that you can pay copywriters to do for you. But no one thinks and writes exactly like you. However well you brief a writer, their words will never be precisely what you are thinking. If you aren't confident about spelling or grammar, it may be useful to pay someone to check and correct your copy. But I urge you to at least prepare a first draft of anything that will carry your name (or byline, as we journalists say), so that the essence of it remains *yours*.

For many people, their first attempts at online copy come in the form of a blog. So let's take some time to consider why you should write a blog, and how to make it popular.

Why Blog?

Blogging is just like writing a diary, except that anyone on the internet can read it. For some people, blogging has become almost a way of life, and they define themselves as bloggers above all else. However, there are millions of blogs out there, most of them unread. So why bother? What makes the difference between success and failure?

1. Blogs that provide **useful advice** will be followed by potential customers, who will refer them on to their friends. It's another way of **raising your profile** and promoting your brand. If you are seen as an expert who constantly provides practical advice, you will become trusted, and people buy from those they trust. If your blog becomes known as a centre of expertise and debate for your sector, you will benefit from the credibility that it gives, as well as receiving valuable ideas and feedback. Some of the most popular blogs are read by tens of thousands of people, and can act as opinion formers within an industry. Because of the simplicity and speed of production, news can break on a blog before it is seen or heard anywhere else. This is part of the phenomenon known as citizen journalism.

    But there is a downside too. Because the majority of blogs are the work of one person, they may consist of opinions or rumours masquerading as verified facts. If your blog is to be seen as credible, you should take as much care as a journalist publishing an article in a magazine, particularly since the laws of libel still apply.

2. You can use your blog not only to **promote your brand**, but also to **protect** it. If a crisis occurs, you need to establish yourself as the main source of information. Your blog can act as a focus for customers and journalists alike. Not only that, if you allow comments (as you should, in my view), you will see instantly the concerns that are being raised, and be able to move quickly to deal with them. However, don't feel the need to respond personally to

every critical comment on your blog. You will find that other readers will often post comments that deal with the issue for you. In addition, there are some mischievous individuals who will post provocative comments simply to start a debate, which if you enter into, you will never win. You do need to keep an eye out for obscene or potentially libellous comments, however, and delete them as soon as you can.

3. Regular blogging gets you into the **habit of writing often**, which is essential if you ever want to write a book or anything else of length. Let's assume you write a blog every day of 250 words. Ten blogs (2,500 words) can be pulled together into a special report. Four special reports (10,000 words) make a good sized eBook (delivered electronically, like a word-processing file). Four eBooks (40,000 words) make a real book. If you've been paying attention, you will realise that in 10 x 4 x 4 days (160 days, or about six months, allowing for a bit of time off), you can have written a book by doing nothing more than blogging. So, if you write a daily blog of 250 words, you can turn out two books a year.

What Should I Put in My Blog?

The most obvious answer is **engaging content**.

If you want people to leave with a good impression, you must provide something of value. Your blog has to be interesting, but more importantly, must give the reader something they can use, or something they can think about. You can include video, pictures, audio or text, but all of it needs to be there for a reason. It is very important, as in all forms of communication, to consider the needs of your audience. However fascinating you may find pictures of pre-war doorstops, unless you have an audience that likes them too, it is pointless including them in your blog.

The easiest way to find out what works for your audience is to watch the comments you receive. They will tell you what is important to your readers, and you should heed what they say.

If people read blogs at all, it is unlikely that they will pay attention to more than five on a regular basis. Given the choice of millions, you need to think carefully about how you can make your blog a must-read.

Engaging content is valuable, inspiring or thought-provoking (hopefully all three). You must be **interested in what you write**, otherwise your readers will move on. Ideally, you should not be just interested, but **passionate**. Your passion will come through in the way you express yourself, and you will develop a loyal following. Despite the importance of Google-friendly text, never forget that you are writing a blog for real people to read, not for search engines to crawl over.

Check your content carefully for **spelling** and **grammar** before you post it. I don't know about you, but when I find simple spelling errors, or badly-written sentences, I am distracted from the meaning of the content. Ideally, ask someone to proofread your postings for you. If you can't find anyone handy, try the trick of reading them out loud. You will be surprised at how easy it is to spot any errors.

Give yourself **plenty of time** to write your blog postings. A post which has been dashed off in a hurry will be obvious, and can indicate a lack of respect for your readers. If you are keen to post some breaking news, you can always add a couple of sentences to make your point, and indicate that you will expand the post when you have more time or information.

Remember that some people will be visiting your blog for the first time. You should offer them something too. I recommend that you create a **guide for first-timers**, including links to important posts, **outlining your philosophy**. Make sure that this guide is visible on every page of your blog by including a box about it in the sidebar.

To help all readers, both new and experienced, to navigate your blog, you can create another box in the sidebar which **links to popular posts**, or those you are particularly proud of. This will help people to understand your point of view, and will save them from having to search for the really good stuff (yes, I know, it's all good stuff, but some of it, I'm sure, is especially brilliant).

Within your blog posts, include links to other posts, other sites, or definitions of terms that may not be obvious. Your readers will appreciate this.

What About Look and Feel?

You will have the choice of some basic designs from your blog host. Most also allow you to customise the appearance reasonably extensively. For a fee, you can seek out a designer and have a design made to order. Whether you go this far is up to you. At the very least, you need a well-chosen logo, font and colours to give your blog its own identity.

Do I Have to Write My Blog Myself?

If you're busy, you may consider employing someone else to write blog posts for you. There are a number of large corporations that have gone down this route. A note of caution – if your ghost-writer is pretending to be you, and the subterfuge is discovered, it's bad PR. The simple rule I suggest is that if it has your name on it, the words should be yours, even if they are dictated rather than typed in. If it is a corporate blog, it doesn't matter so much, but putting by-lines on each posting is a nice touch.

Can I Make Money from My Blog?

In short, with difficulty. If you want to use your blog as a direct money-making operation, you need to work hard and learn the techniques described elsewhere in this book.

Indirectly, your blog can lead to a more profitable business, by establishing you as an expert, but don't expect people to pay for blog content. I would also advise against having relevant adverts down the side of your blog, since they not only distract from the content, they produce very small returns.

One more thing. Don't call it a blog, since that can put people off. I call my blog *The Media Coach Report*. It sounds friendlier, and attracts more readers.

Finally, some tips to take away . . .

8 General Blogging Tips

1. Blog every day (OK, you can take Sunday off).

2. Blog early in the day to get it done.

3. Link to it from your site.

4. Encourage people to comment.

5. Add extra features (such as video links, Twitter feeds).

6. Use pictures occasionally.

7. Think about your audience. Write for them.

8. If you don't enjoy writing it, don't do it.

15 Ways to Make Your Content More Shareable

Social networking is all about sharing. You will build and maintain a following if you share great content, and if you produce great content that others enjoy reading and sharing. Here are a few tips to make your content ready-to-share . . .

1. **Keep it simple and short.** A couple of paragraphs are more likely to be shared than a 1500-word article. It can be more difficult to write a short piece than a long one. Mark Twain is alleged to have said to a newspaper editor: *"I didn't have time to write a short letter, so I wrote a long one instead."*

2. **Make it relevant.** If you can link it to a hot news story, people will pass it on. Make a habit of listening to the news headlines everyday, or scanning the headlines on a news website. Whenever you see anything that can be related to your business, write a few paragraphs and post on your blog or favourite social media site. It will take only a few minutes, but as well as attracting the attention of potential customers, it may also win you a call from a reporter.

3. **Address a common need.** For example, a piece titled 'How to win more business' is almost guaranteed to get people clicking and

reading. Think about the things that you wanted to know as your business began and grew. Those are the same things that everyone thinks about, so offer advice based on your experience.

4. **Be controversial.** No one wants to share a post that agrees with the majority view. For example, many people believe that the best way to win more business is to have as large a network as possible. Why not write an article under the heading 'How to halve the size of your network and double the value of your business' (if you don't know how to do that, drop me a line!).

5. **Use lists**, such as 'Seven tips for a better Facebook business page'. We're in a list right now. Look back a few paragraphs. This section is called '15 Tips to Make Your Content More Shareable'. You are reading it. See how it works?

6. **Create a stunning headline.** All journalists know that the headline is the most important part of a story. It initially catches your eye, then engages your interest before leading you into the story, Next time you read a newspaper (these are folded piles of paper with typing on them, available at any newsagent), notice that you don't read every word. Instead, you scan through the headlines, looking for something that catches your interest. Then you read the whole story.

7. **Mention a celebrity** e.g. 'Five presentation tips from Steve Jobs'. This needs a bit of care. You need to pick the right celebrity for the topic you're writing about. No one would be likely to read 'Lady Gaga's guide to accounting software for small businesses'.

8. **Appeal to emotions** e.g. 'How to feel good about cold-calling'. This can work particularly well if you invoke a negative emotion, such as 'How to overcome the fear of speaking to large audiences'. If you can put people in touch with their emotions, they are much more likely to read what you have to say.

9. **Give it a tweetable title.** That means fewer than 120 characters, not the Twitter limit of 140. Remember that you need to leave

people room to add their recommendation to your comment, even if it's "This is great".

10. **Respond to a well-read article.** If you take a counter-view to a widely seen piece, it could gain attention. This is one of the lesser-used techniques to encourage people to read and share your content. However strongly you disagree with an article, always stay polite. Use positive arguments to win the day. Do not ever make fun of someone, patronise them, or use bad language. You lose the argument immediately. Even if the original author is rude to you, never insult them back. Stay calm.

11. **Respond to comments on your articles.** People love a good debate, especially if the author takes part. Your participation will be unexpected, which makes it all the more interesting.

12. **Alert opinion-formers.** Send links to people who already have large followings. It can take only one comment from a well-followed expert to generate a big audience reading your material.

13. **Tell a story which makes a general, useful point.** In the world of professional speaking, which I inhabit for around half my working time, there's a classic story structure, which is: tell a story; make a point; give the audience a practical example they can use. The last part is critical (and often overlooked by storytellers), since that is what makes content 'sticky' and unforgettable.

14. **Don't over-promote your products or services.** That may sound an odd thing to say in a book about internet marketing. What I mean is that an article which is obviously created for the sole purpose of selling is not going to be shared. Nor is a piece that mentions your SEO keywords in every sentence.

15. **Encourage people to share.** Include a call to action in the content – 'Why not share this?' sounds almost too obvious, but it works.

It's all about delivering consistent, high-quality content There are two aspects to this (obviously) – consistency and quality. It's no use posting a large volume of material once every few weeks. Little and often is much better. It needs to stand out, so quality is vital. 'How-to' lists work well (see above).

Finally, a word of caution. In a sense, we're all publishers these days. There are good and bad things about that. Recent court cases have demonstrated the dangers of posting opinions on social networks. You can be held liable for anything you say, especially about another person, or if you breach discrimination laws.

Journalists understand the rules of publishing, and what you can and cannot say. Additionally, there is a journalistic code of conduct which guides behaviour.

Here are some key elements of the code of conduct that journalists abide by, a useful guide to online postings too:

- differentiate between fact and opinion

- avoid plagiarism

- strive to ensure that information disseminated is honestly conveyed, accurate and fair

- produce no material likely to lead to hatred or discrimination

- do nothing to intrude into anybody's private life, grief or distress.

In short, you need to be aware that when you are posting content online, even in closed groups, you are publishing information, and you must consider the potential impact of your words. You can still be opinionated, controversial and challenging (in fact, this will make your comments more widely read), but you must also remember your responsibilities. Not only are we all publishers, we're all journalists too.

Now put this book down for a moment (there are plenty more great chapters to read soon), and type a few paragraphs about something that you want to share online. I guarantee in 15 minutes, you will have produced something unique and valuable. Do it every day.

EMAIL MARKETING

by Jamie Gledhill

About Jamie Gledhill

JAMIE GLEDHILL is co-founder and managing director of Emailmovers (**www.emailmovers.com**), one of the UK's leading email marketing agencies. With over ten years' industry experience, Jamie provides the drive and insight to propel the company along its consistent growth path whilst maintaining his vision to help businesses communicate with their customers more effectively by email.

Why Email?

WHY EMAIL? This is an obvious question but one that is, for whatever reason, often overlooked by companies.

Let it be said from the outset that email marketing is not a universal panacea to marketing ills. Rarely can it replace all other forms of marketing. But it sits nicely alongside more traditional methods, offering highly cost-effective returns when implemented correctly.

A common mistake is to compare this with, say, Google's cost-per-click (CPC) model. This is an impractical comparison as one is not comparing like with like. A CPC campaign will bring you traffic that is looking for your product or service. Email, however, takes an opportunity that your business or product provides and presents it to your target audience. A world of difference, but the two models may co-exist very well and together cover a wider base.

Before you begin, it is important to establish what you expect to gain from an email marketing campaign. There are many reasons to contact other companies via email; below are just a few. Some of these are blatantly obvious, others have more subtle implications:

- Sales prospecting – relatively easy to understand and launch.
- Compliance – traditionally gets a good result; shock tactics can be useful.

- Brand building – difficult to measure; generally, more is better.

- Newsletter – useful in nurturing and retention.

- Questionnaire – notoriously low returns; need very careful planning and implementation; usually only a one-off chance so extra care needed.

Each of the above requires a different pitch. For example, a sales retention email would be pitched entirely differently to a prospecting email.

Newsletters are a very important part of the mix, often neglected because of the amount of work involved. Aside from the obvious promotion benefits they can also play a part in your SEO work, in the invitation of feedback (good and bad) and countless other areas of your marketing.

If you haven't started a newsletter yet, then do so. If you already have one then resolve to spend some more time each month looking for content. It will reap rewards in terms of customer engagement.

Aims and Expectations

It is crucial to set realistic goals before beginning any email campaign. These can then be used as a benchmark to measure performance. In practice, this may not be as easy as it sounds – each type of campaign will have different expectations.

Useful measurements are open rates (how many people open/read an email) and click rates (how many of these actually click a link within an email).

Open rates

Open rates are usually expressed as a percentage. To arrive at the figure use the formula $OR = (ER \div ED) \times 100$

where

OR=open rate

ER=emails read

ED=emails delivered

e.g. *(5196 ÷ 65,000) × 100 = 8% open rate*

Click rates

As above but usually expressed as a percentage of the emails opened. Use the formula $CR = (EC \div ER) \times 100$

where

CR=click rate

EC=emails clicked

ER=emails read

e.g. *(265 ÷ 5196) × 100 = 5%*

If the email is sales-orientated then the return on investment (ROI) is a relatively simple calculation. Calculating ROI on other types of email (e.g. brand-building newsletters) is far more complicated.

Often it pays to 'reverse engineer' your proposal to deduce the degree of activity necessary to generate sales to the required level. Let's take a specific example . . .

Campaign aim – to sell widgets

The profit margin is £10 per widget.

Assumed rates: 10% open rate, 5% click, 10% conversion to sale.

To sell 50 widgets:

50 × 10 = 500 clicks

500 × 20 = 10,000 opens

10,000 × 10 = 100,000 emails to broadcast

So we calculate the list at potentially 100,000 emails to realise projected sales. Of course, we would need to source the data at no more than £5.00CPM (cost per thousand) to realise this and break even. Based on these figures, the campaign is likely to fail in strict **ROI** terms.

There are obvious possible remedies.

- **Increase the profit margin per item**. This is often possible, especially if moving from traditional retail to online sales. Overheads are substantially lowered and thus the profit margin increases without touching the price.

- **Increase the open and click rates**. This is very much a trial-and-error, suck-it-and-see methodology. Try varying the subject line and rephrasing the copy.

Never be content to rest on your laurels. The old adage says "If it isn't broken, don't fix it". In email marketing we can ignore this. The emailing landscape changes *very* quickly and evolution is the key to success.

Of course, there may be times when you just need to admit that perhaps the world isn't quite ready to buy into your product. However one wraps it, a dead donkey will always be just that.

Too often companies complain that they have a fantastic open rate combined with a decent click rate, but few if any sales. If we compare this to being a shopkeeper, it becomes easier to understand. If you had a shop with a footfall of, say, 800 customers a day, with just two or three daily sales, then you obviously have a problem.

- You are too expensive

    or

- your goods are inferior

    or

- the demand just isn't there

    or

- a combination of these factors

In the example above, the most drastic cure is to drive thousands more people through your shop. However, this means sourcing an ever-increasing volume of emails and leads to . . .

The leaky bucket syndrome

"Email marketing can be like trying to fill a bucket with holes in it," says Mark Brownlow in his email marketing report (**tinyurl.com/leakybucketemail**). "And email marketers fall into two schools of thought on how to do so.

"The old school tackles the problem by using more water and pouring faster. It's inefficient and dooms you to a never-ending game of catch-up and costs. (And eventually you run out of water.) The new school plugs the holes.

"The old email marketing is volume-oriented. At its worst, the old email marketing sees email addresses as a commodity. [That's] the thinking behind this quote (overheard at a recent event):

"I just bought 4 million email addresses. They're not targeted, but . . . (shrug)"

"The old email marketing is short-term. It sees sending more of the same emails, more often, as the answer to falling response rate . . . like an addiction: you need to send more and more to get the same buzz. And like any such addiction, the eventual outcome is not pretty.

"The old email marketing falls prey to blinkered and narrow interests, letting their email program become hijacked by too many conflicting or inappropriate goals or approaches.

"The new email marketing thinks smart email marketing, not bulk email marketing."

Work hard or work smart

Smart marketing today involves engagement. The internet means that you are no longer in local competition – it's a global market and your competitors have just declared open season on you. The days of lazy marketing are over. 'Spray and pray' is dead and buried.

To succeed it is no longer viable to broadcast millions of emails and sit waiting for the phone to ring. You have to get involved and take a far more pro-active sales and marketing stance.

A tried and tested method is that of sales nurturing by email. This enables you to convert prospects to leads, and leads to customers, using a softer approach. Normal methods involve a series of emails that build in importance. The countdown method is also useful, although over-used these days.

- "60 days to the end of our sale"
- "Only 30 days left"
- "Last few days"
- "Final chance".

Email Data

If you have not already, start building an organic email list. Investing in customer relationships is always a smart decision and there are a variety of ways to collect information from your customers. A simple and popular method is to add a sign-up form on your website. Offering incentives to generate sign-ups such as a free report, for example, is also an option. If you are buying an email list be sure the list you purchase is well-targeted to suit your needs and the names have opted-in to receive email messages.

Important considerations

There are three points that are crucial to remember for any email list, whatever its provenance.

De-dupe – short for de-duplication

This process involves ensuring that email addresses occur only once within any list. It is very easy to get duplicate addresses in a list, especially when working with aggregated data formed by combining two or more lists. Failing to perform a de-duping will result in a recipient receiving two or more copies of the same email. They won't thank you for it.

This procedure should always be performed on any new list, as well as after additions or updates are made to it.

Unsubs – short for unsubscribe request

Best practice requires that you offer an unsubscribe option along with each email broadcast – needless to say, any removal requests submitted should be honoured. Normal practice is to maintain a suppression list against which lists are screened prior to broadcast. Most broadcast solutions will support this as an automatic feature, otherwise you are left with the manual option.

This should be given all due diligence. Nothing is likely to cause you more problems than not letting people unsubscribe. Get it wrong and your world explodes!

Always be prepared to deal with 'forwarded emails'. A recipient receives your email at say john@anyco.com . However, he has an active forward command on this address and all emails are automatically forwarded to jb@hotmail.com. Subsequent unsubscribe requests are pointless if received from the latter address, as the former is still the active address within your data set.

Cleansing

Failure to maintain your list and remove hard bounces (an email message that has been rejected and returned to the sender because the email address is invalid or does not exist) will cause you tremendous problems in the long run. ISPs are extremely sensitive to the number of bounces recorded against a specific IP address. Repeat offenders are just digging their own graves. Worst-case scenario – you could end up on a blacklist as a 'spammer'.

Keeping your data current is possibly the hardest task of all. Many companies try applying a tele-verification model, literally calling each contact in an attempt to verify their details. This is at best slow and inefficient. Given the 'churn' within today's job market it is also akin to the proverbial painting of the Forth Bridge, i.e. never-ending.

Customer/prospect engagement can really assist here. If you are on good emailing terms with the contacts in your list then frequent 'soft' reminders should prompt a large percentage of them to update their details with you. No list can ever be 100% accurate and the percentage accuracy always falls in line with the list volume.

In summary – keep your lists as clean and current as possible.

The Email Design

Consideration must be given to the type of email desired and its aim: to reach prospects, retain customers or build awareness. Style and technique will vary accordingly. As always, this is subjective but a quick read of emails currently in your inbox should suffice to outline the major differences.

Design elements

Layout

Keep your layouts simple and try not to use complicated structures; they are likely to render incorrectly in most email clients. Two columns are easier to read than one continuous scroll. Always ensure the maximum page width is only 600 pixels.

Images

Keep images to a minimum (preferably a 70:30 ratio of text to image) and slice up any large images into sections placed in their own table. Never use background images, as many email clients will ignore them; use background colours instead. Remember, email providers can sometimes block images so do not include important content in them without an <alt> tag.

CTAs

Always include plenty of calls to action (CTAs) – phone number, reply address and hyperlinks to sites, brochures, forms etc. A CTA is most effective above-the-fold (i.e. near the beginning of the email) and can be text or image-based.

Social media

Email is an excellent channel to engage prospective and existing customers – but why stop at email? On every email you send, include a link to your social media pages so that companies and individuals interested in your products and services can receive updates via various different channels.

View online

As email clients tend to deal with HTML code in varying ways your email may not appear exactly as you have designed it on all systems. In extreme examples clients will have the HTML system disabled and are thus likely to view your 'oh so' carefully designed mailer as pure text, with strings of HTML code embedded and displayed as just that – strings of code.

By adding a 'view online' option, you help the recipient get around this. The link points to a URL where you have hosted the email for just this scenario. This takes the recipient away from the email client entirely and allows for the email to be viewed through their normal web browser.

Forward to a friend

If your broadcast system supports this it can be very useful in boosting readership. Aside from making the task of forwarding the email much simpler for the reader, it also often serves as a subliminal prompt causing them to do just that.

Footer

The footer appears below the email content and is important. Here's where you must offer the option to unsubscribe, your company address and contact information.

Subject lines

The subject line of an email is of prime importance. An incorrect or unwise choice can totally negate any campaign straight off the bat. One should try to write incisive subject lines but within certain guidelines, avoiding the use of obvious spam-trigger words and phrases. Remember the purpose of the subject line – to prompt the recipient to open the email.

There are various online tests for this kind of thing and a quick Google search will find them for you. As always, I don't believe that any single one should be treated as sacrosanct; but they can save hours in the testing procedure.

Content

The text of an email should always be concise and incisive – short, sweet and to the point. This is something of an art form, and can often be contracted out. Bullet points always serve to highlight any USPs that you may possess.

If language and prose is not your forté, then find someone with the necessary skillset. Badly composed emails tend to produce poor results. Please always check grammar and spelling and *always* take a second opinion. It is is to easy to overlook mistakes such as the ones in this sentence. Did you spot them? Your critics will! If time allows, revisit your copy the next day and perform a précis exercise on your own work. You will be surprised at the results.

Remember that your email is often the first point of contact between you and a potential customer, and errors do not impress! You never get a second chance to make a first impression.

Getting Your Email Delivered

Having designed the email, we now need to check that it delivers. Never assume that your email client is a definitive test. Some of the best filters are employed by the 'free' accounts (Hotmail, Gmail etc) so it is best to set up dummy accounts on some of these for testing purposes.

The mechanics of delivery vary between platforms; basic principles, however, hold true across them all. The process invariably consists of the following steps –

- upload the cleansed data file
- upload the creative HTML design
- host all images where necessary – note the use of absolute addresses
- set up the broadcast, stating the subject line
- send the email to test addresses
- *ensure* that the unsub/suppression file is active

You are now on the brink of the point of no return. If anything is wrong, the next step is irreversible. Check your checklist, then check again.

Click *go* – you are now committed and inboxes will start to fill *very* rapidly. It's now a bit too late to find problems.

More sophisticated delivery systems allow for 'throttled' delivery, usually quoted as emails per hour e.g. 5,000, 20,000 etc. Un-throttled, many systems are capable of delivering millions of emails per hour, or around 300 *per second*.

> **GOLDEN RULES**
> - Check your work
> - re-check it
> - seek an alternative 'sanity check' from a third party
> - check again
> - click send.

Complaints

Remember never to take a complaint as personal. Some of the more sensitive amongst us have a tendency to do just that. In some instances this can have repercussions on future performance – e.g. a growing reluctance to answer the phone. To email successfully and pro-actively, you need a slightly thick skin!

It's a fact of life that however careful you are with your emailing activities, you will get complaints. Taking any cross-section of complainers, they will vary from the mildly apologetic to the raving psychopath, with all shades in between.

So, you've sent your email and have picked up some decent business. The sun is shining, all is well with the world . . . and then you get a phone call so loud you have to hold it a foot away from your ear.

Yes, it's a disgruntled recipient of your latest masterpiece, and they are *not* happy. Accusations fly about where you got their address, whether you've broken the law, why you feel it acceptable to spam people. What do you do?

Never, never, never get into a verbal argument with this character. Usually he will be unwilling to listen to reason anyway. Situations like this have a way of escalating in a very short space of time.

If you have taken all the right steps in respect of compliance and permissions, then you occupy the high ground, and, if you like, you can defend it all day long. The only course of action open to you is to follow procedure – take him off your list and confirm this to him by email. Of course, ensure that he doesn't get your next newsletter, or you'll have created a real problem.

> **TIP**
> When unsubscribing angry recipients, it usually pays dividends to search your data lists for any other addresses registered at the same domain (provided it is a personal domain and not something like **Gmail.com**!) and remove those at the same time. This should sever all ties with a potential time-bomb.

If the email list has been purchased, then refer the matter to your supplier.

Implement a procedure in-house for dealing with complaints and un-subs. You will save countless hours of potential fire-fighting. Ensure that you are *au fait* with the legislation. If in doubt, always visit the official website of the Information Commissioner's Office (**www.ico.gov.uk**), the watchdog for the entire industry.

Always be aware of the difference between **corporate** and **consumer** email addresses. These are two very different animals and *must* always be treated differently.

Tracking

So, the email has gone. You looked at the project, costed it out, weighed up all the pros and cons, designed and tested the flyer, set the job ready on the broadcast server and finally, finally summoned the resolve to click the mouse and commit to broadcast.

What now? It's been ten minutes and your phone still hasn't rung. Have the emails actually been sent out? Is anybody reading them? Has anyone clicked a link to your website? Just how exactly do you collate these results?

Broadcast platforms will vary in how these figures are presented. Use an agency and you should receive a full and comprehensive report some 24 hours later. Use an online solution and things are better – results may be available in real-time, but in any case within an hour.

OK, so far so good. But let's now be a little pro-active. It would be great if we could see those who read the email as they do so. Why? Well, what better time to call them, now that you have an electronic foot-in-the-door.

If using your own customer relationship management (CRM) then the process is:

- record the response
- call or email the reader
- establish the interest level
- nurture accordingly.

Every reader that is ignored is a potential lost sale.

Next Step

If your original aims and expectations have been reached, fantastic. If not, it could be down to a number of factors. The key to successful email marketing is testing, making changes, using what works and dropping what doesn't.

As we have learnt, the emailing landscape changes very quickly and evolution is the key to success. Hopefully this chapter has helped you begin to master it.

MARKETING WITH YOUTUBE

by Filip Matous

About Filip Matous

FILIP MATOUS is a digital strategist who can be found on Twitter at @filipmatous or on **EvergreenReputation.com**, a company he cofounded.

Small and medium-sized enterprises (SMEs) that start using YouTube as part of their marketing mix often focus on the wrong metrics for business success. All too often, YouTube newbies focus on the viewer count. "The more views, the better! A slick video is what we need, blasted through some social media channels; let's get viral!"

Most likely you won't go viral. And, as an SME, view count is one of the *worst* metrics to use if your business objectives are based on wanting to increase sales or gain warm leads.

First, allow me to briefly introduce myself and why I was asked contribute my insights on YouTube (which I will use interchangeably with the term online video). I've been working with many forms of digital marketing since starting in a public relations agency in 2007. When I began, I was surprised that most clients would be very happy when we won them a story in a national paper with a readership of 250,000 but were not so excited when a blogger with a relevant niche audience of 10,000 ran a blog post on them. Yet in many cases the niche blogger brought them much higher quality traffic than a newspaper ever could. As I started using online video I saw similar praise of traditional media views and confusion when it came to online video views. Earlier this year a prospective client for a software company asked me to source them some people to make a viral ninja video with their branding. I couldn't see what ninjas had to do with their product and suggested that if all they were after were views and popularity we should just make an epic cat video. For SMEs, high view counts may correlate with, but don't *cause*, high sales.

If your marketing mix calls for it, YouTube can be a strong arrow in your quiver, useful for hitting warm leads, fresh sales and increased reputation. But YouTube marketing, by itself, shouldn't be your whole marketing plan. Rather, YouTube is a tool you can employ to deliver results. If there are no clear business goals, making a snazzy video won't do much for you other than waste your time and money.

So, let's explore two very common SME business objectives and the strategies for how you can use video as a tool to make them happen. Then we'll look at the technical bits on how to actually create a video at the end of the chapter.

Objective #1: Increase Reputation Within a Niche

One straightforward way to gain a good reputation is to interact with leaders and media in your niche. Let's use the word *influencers* as an umbrella term for people who have influence in your business area, whether they are in media or well-respected thought leaders.

Say you are a business that sells blue cheese and you want to attract the attention of the cheese-buying connoisseur. Now, there will be cheese trade magazines with journalists, bloggers who review and use fancy cheese, and other places online where cheese is discussed. Perhaps some other brands of blue cheese have an existing reputation that you can learn from and see who they network with. Connecting to a mix of these influencers can bring new buyers to your brand by building your reputation. And video can be the specific tool to bring you together.

So how does a video allow you to achieve your objective: connecting to influencers who can bring you potential buyers?

How about creating a video around a topic that your niche is currently debating or discussing. Or you can film a timely video response to an issue that's hot. Perhaps find a way to interview an influencer. Don't just create a video that puts your name and brand front and centre. The point is to mix in your expertise without being artificial.

Think about it. Which of the following do you trust more?

- Ads in a magazine *or* the non-advertorial articles?

- Event sponsors who pay to have their brand on display *or* the thought leaders who are paid to speak?

- The commercials on TV *or* the brands that actually appear in TV shows?

- A video ad on a sales page *or* a YouTube video that a blogger you trust recommends?

It's the second option each time, because they're not paid for – at least not directly. **Earned media** is what you are after if you want reputation. A video in a non-salesy tone suggests you don't have to pay for exposure because you are an expert; your products or services are worth talking about.

Strategy

So, how do you get your approach right?

It starts with making sure you have a thought-out plan for what happens once you film and edit the video. Who do you want seeing the video, what action should they take after watching it? Will you just post it on YouTube or on your company blog? On someone else's website? Who will help you share it? Do you have any existing networks, say on LinkedIn, that would welcome the video? Perhaps access to a relevant email list? Don't skip these questions or chances are the video will fail.

How do you find relevant influencers to connect with?

First be clear on who you are after. Once you've identified the right kind of audience that you want to reach, create a wish list. I learned a simple way to do this when I worked in New York on the launch of a new Monopoly game. It's a common public relations practice: the media list.

Use Excel or Google Docs to create a list of influencers you want to get involved. The list should as a minimum have the following columns: name, website, rough readership count, Twitter handle, phone, email and notes.

Often the following will feature:

- Media/websites with specific contact names
- Niche bloggers, thought leaders and journalists
- Potential clients/partners
- Trade events/conferences

Usually once I have about 100 different names and publications I break them into three different tiers: the star influencers, the moderately influential and the enthusiasts.

The first-tier *star influencers* are usually around a dozen names that I've thoroughly researched online and really want to connect with. If they are a blogger or journalist I'll read through what they publish online and think about how to make it worth their time to be involved with the project. If they use Twitter, I see what they like tweeting about. If they speak at events I'll look at what topics they cover. Once I have at least a decent understanding of who they are I'll carefully craft some form of soft pitch (email, tweet, phone call etc.) to these dozen – with a well-thought-out action I want them to take.

Resist the urge to make a less time-intensive generic pitch to these people. They need tailored communication that makes it clear how they, specifically, will benefit from being involved in the video you are creating and why their audience or personal brand will benefit from being involved. This works like it would if you were asking for an audio/print interview. A well-thought-out video should really provide value to them, so there's no need to bluff.

For the second-tier, *moderate influencers*, spend less time on this communication but still make it personal. Use their names in emails and do your research; just don't invest loads of time, as your main focus should be tier one.

For the third tier, *enthusiasts*, if time allows try to be personal, but as there is usually never enough time, a generic email outlining in a couple lines what the video project is about should suffice. The more generic the communication, the worse the response rate; that's why it is so important to prioritise who gets to be tier one and receives most of your attention.

Sometimes the creation of the media list influences the angle that your video project takes. It can help the content or approach be more relevant and timely, because you'll have fresh experience of exactly what your niche influencers are discussing right now.

Reputation-building videos are ideal for:

- growing relationships with influencers
- positioning you/your company as a thought leader
- generating warm leads
- creating a reason to talk with desired customers or clients without having to sell.

Personal example

I had a client in property development who wanted a reputation in a very specific location, with a very specific community: other property developers and property media.

So he commissioned a video with a dozen other influencers from that specific geographic location. Part of the brief was to be one of the contributors to the informative, non-sales video about property in the region – but not to focus on him as the main person or company financially backing the video/website.

The video and its release was through a white-label info website we built (essentially non-branded content) and the dozen influencers agreed to appear on film because it helped get their expertise out to others and it was about a topic they cared about.

Result? Although the video was only viewed by just over 5,000 people in the property industry, it achieved the client's brief: to gain reputation as being one of the big players in the space. Would it make sense to try to get millions of views on this kind of video? No. There are only so many people in the space.

The client was able to gain better relationships with other influencers and network naturally during the film launch event. Awareness and business deals resulted from the new relationships.

Of the dozen influencers, some were media, some were experts, and some were people the client wanted to have business relationships with. It was a win-win for all involved.

Objective #2: Humanise Your Company

Want to add the human touch online? Right now thousands of companies are convinced that writing this line, *"we are passionate about what we do"* (575,000 Google results) or *"we believe in being transparent"* (82,500 results) will somehow win over a reader. But when was the last time you read someone saying he was passionate and thought he really was? Shouldn't passion radiate without having to be claimed? That's where video can come in. Video is a great way to show, not tell, visitors what your business is and why it matters to you.

Personality matters. But how many websites tell you to contact info@companyname.com instead of a specific person? I often encounter SMEs who fear to make the team visible on the site in case it makes the business look too small. Employees writing on the site use words like *we* when they should use *I*. This isn't the best approach if you want to demonstrate passion and transparency. Instead, embrace the size of your company. Don't stress the employee count, just focus on letting your personality show. Be proud that you are a small, efficient team or sole trader. Allow people to buy into you.

Video blogging is one of the best ways to pull back the curtain and invite people into your business. Here are some points worth considering before you try video blogging:

1. Do you see the opportunities in being known as a thought leader in your niche?

2. Is there something you're an expert in? Do people ask you about something professionally? Is there anything that irritates you in your industry? Is there anything that fires you up?

3. Do you have any specific person or community in mind whose attention you'd like to catch?

4. What is your current least-effective marketing effort and could you pause it to try three months of video blogging? Say, once a week?

If you are able to answer those four questions positively, we can get cracking.

What we're going to be doing is (1) developing your personal brand, (2) harnessing your expertise, (3) crafting an idea to communicate to a specific audience and (4) committing to a regular video blogging schedule.

The main problem areas to bear in mind when video blogging are:

- **Length.** Try to answer one question in less than two minutes. The drop off in viewers when a video goes past two minutes on YouTube is very high.

- **Focus.** Find one specific detail or question and stay on topic.

- **Sales talk.** Drop the sales! Seriously, just focus on giving value and stop worrying about giving too much value for free. If people start seeing you as a thought leader worth listening to, some of them will turn into customers and clients. I wouldn't have a career if this didn't work.

- **Stop telling.** Show you are a passionate expert. Don't ever call yourself one. Just prove it. Let the self-appointed gurus drop away; they always do.

- **Audience.** Make sure a specific viewer is in your mind when crafting the post. Don't imagine too broad an audience and attempt to address it. Talk to someone by their name if suitable. Perhaps say 'Sally from [town or site] asks [question] . . .' in the video. If the question is good, other people have surely also thought about asking it.

Once you have recorded your video blog, besides posting it on YouTube and your company blog, send it directly to the intended audience or individual you had in mind when you made the video.

Chances are they will take notice because it is crafted for them. Great business is built off the back of good conversation like this.

Three Other Online Video Ideas

1. Influencer vox pops

Influencers will be speaking at trade shows and events. Ask them for a quick interview during the event. Or even email them before the event asking them for a few minutes on the day. It's often easy to grab them after they finish their speaking session. Find a quiet spot or have a lapel microphone ready. Chances are that they will share the video once you put it online and show them where it is.

2. Event round-up vox pops

This is a great way to extend the publicity of an event you run after it ends. Interview key attendees to get their thoughts about the event and ask them what their number one lesson from it was. You can then post the videos online over the next few weeks.

When you post the vox pops online, email the people you interviewed to let them know it's online, thank them and almost always they will help you share the video without you needing to ask.

3. Video reviews

What types of content does your niche consume? Trade magazines, books, videos? I like reviewing new books or exploring the authors behind them as most authors are hungry for reviews and take notice when someone reviews their book. I don't suggest you lie and fake positivity about what you read. Say what you really think about things you really like. The content that you enjoy can act as a great way to get on an author's radar.

Technical Points About Video

The two most common problems with video are sound and lighting. Dark faces and noisy, low quality audio are the consistent double-barrel destroyers of otherwise great video.

At the very least I suggest if you are going to do the filming yourself you invest in a good microphone, LED light panel and tripod.

Sound

RØDE (**www.rodemic.com**) shotgun mics are decent for interviews if there isn't much background noise. Check if your video camera or video-capable digital camera has a line-in microphone. If there is no line-in jack, opt for a microphone like the Zoom H1 (**www.zoom.co.jp/english/products/h1**) or H4 (**www.zoom.co.jp/english/products/h4**). Decent microphones usually start at £65 like the H1 (it is good, albeit fiddly).

TIP

Ask everyone within a five-metre radius of the filming to turn off their mobile phones. The mobile signal frequency often jams the microphone with a *'vrrr vrrr'* sound. You can often hear this sound at events or by laying your mobile phone too close to speakers.

Lighting

Even a cheap £30 unbranded LED light panel from eBay can do wonders for bringing out subjects' faces when there is a lack of bright light or a strong background light but low foreground lighting.

Scout out where you are filming; if it's indoors, watch out for fluorescent lights. They can turn into a flickering nightmare once recorded. If you must record with florescent lights nearby, capture some sample video and play it back to see if there is a telling flicker. If so, you really need to find somewhere else to film as flicker is usually impossible to remove, even with fancy editing software, and can render video unwatchable.

Video camera

The choice of camera depends on what your goal is.

Do you want a simple video with you or someone else talking? An iPhone/iPad + microphone + tripod + good lighting can be perfect. Sometimes if you are doing some quick feedback/commentary a webcam can do the trick.

However, once you get into interview-style videos or just want better production values, digital single-lens reflex cameras (DSLRs) are a great choice. I really like the Canon T3i because it's around £300 and has a nice swivel screen that let's you see what you are filming from many angles (especially useful for filming yourself).

With DSLRs, most lenses can achieve a blurry background and crisp foreground to give footage a cinematic touch. Unfortunately DSLRs typically have a maximum of about ten to 15 minutes' continuous HD recording time. Not ideal for filming talks, though this is something that is quickly being resolved with new technology.

The main perk to using DSLRs is that they are smaller than proper video cameras and produce better looking video. They can also be used to snap stills. A whole episode of *House* was filmed on a Canon 5D and Hollywood is starting to use DSLRs in movies, including recent hits like *The Avengers*.

Software

For editing video on a Mac, iMovie is a good starting place and free. The PC equivalent, Movie Maker, is free and good for basic editing. I personally recommend Final Cut Pro for the Mac if you decide to spend *serious* time with video. Adobe's Premier is a professional set-up if you use a PC.

If you plan on recording Skype video chats or need to record anything on your computer screen, ScreenFlow is a great option.

Online video hosting options

Even though YouTube is often the right choice, sometimes paid options are worth considering. Here are the ins and outs of the two main options: YouTube and Vimeo Pro.

YouTube

The pros of YouTube are that it is free, easy to share and embed in websites, and great for mobile. The cons are that the YouTube logo will always brand your videos and the control you have over your video is not as great as some paid options.

YouTube is a vehicle for Google to sell ads. You have an option to add ads to your videos for profit but I strongly suggest you don't. Adding ads to a B2B video backfires because it can annoy your visitors, looks cheap and you need an enormous number of views to make it worthwhile. YouTube pays between 60p and £3 per 1,000 views. Considering many B2B videos don't even break 100 views, it's not worth it. To make between £600 and £3,000 you need at least 1 million views.

YouTube can be good for traffic but remember that 50 hours of video is uploaded to YouTube every minute. Making your video stand out by relying on YouTube to supply viewers is a bad move.

Vimeo Pro

At £125 per year, Vimeo Pro is a great choice if you want more control over your videos. You can remove the Vimeo logo and replace it with your own. The analytics show far more detail on visitors than YouTube does. It also shows how many people went to your page with the video but didn't press play.

Vimeo also has a free version but it is not open to commercial videos and doesn't provide the control that the paid version gives. If you are going to go for a free platform, stick with YouTube.

Other alternatives exist, such as Wistia at £60 a month, which has more bells and whistles; but for most companies YouTube or Vimeo Pro is the right choice.

LINKEDIN FOR REFERRALS

by Andy Lopata

About Andy Lopata

ANDY LOPATA is a business networking expert who works with companies on how to use networking tools to develop their businesses. He has a regular blog in *The Huffington Post* and is the author of *Recommended: How to Sell Through Networking and Referrals* (Financial Times Prentice Hall), as well as the co-author of two other books on networking.

When not networking, speaking or training, he has the dubious pleasure of being an avid Charlton Athletic football fan.

www.lopata.co.uk

WHEN I WAS in my 20s I worked in a lot of jobs that required cold calling. Jobs ranged from selling raffle tickets to people at home when I backpacked in Australia, to reaching out to the senior executives of major global corporations, to selling advertising space in high-end publications.

Whatever I was selling, and to whomever I was selling, there was one golden rule. I couldn't tell anyone, other than the person I had been tasked to ring, what my call was about. They were the decision-makers. If I started explaining my call to anyone else, the decision would be made on their behalf.

And it would always be 'No'.

That made cold calling an art, and an exercise in patience. It might take several calls to get through to the decision-maker. I would have to build rapport and trust with the receptionist, the PA or the spouse (the *gatekeeper* as we used to call them) while never giving away enough for them to make a decision on my sale.

When I'd finally get through to the decision-maker (by no means guaranteed), I'd then have to convince them to listen to me, to engage in conversation and, ultimately, to buy my product or service.

My experiences back in my 20s are borne out by the experience of so many cold callers today. A Brighton-based marketing firm, Hot to Trot Marketing, surveyed 20 telemarketing agencies with around 1,500 staff between them. They asked the cold callers how many attempts it would take them to get through to a decision-maker. The results were quite startling.

Back in 2007 it was a pretty difficult 10. This rose in 2008 to 18, and in 2009 to 29. *In 2010 it was 41.*

Meanwhile, Scottish firm Market Transformations surveyed 100 CEOs across the UK and discovered that 73% of them won't accept an inbound cold call.[1] Interestingly, in the Market Transformations survey, the same respondents still expected their own staff to make cold calls despite being unwilling to accept such approaches themselves!

In short, cold calling can be a costly, time-consuming and ultimately frustrating exercise. I still believe that it has its place in the marketing mix, but too often businesses turn to a telephone directory before they turn to the most valuable asset they have: their network.

The Power of Networks

In his book, *The Start-up of You*,[2] Reid Hoffman, the founder of the social networking website LinkedIn, says that the "best way to engage new people is via *the people you know*".

He's right.

I don't cold call any more. I still ring decision-makers and I'm still greeted by their PAs. But I no longer have to convince them to put me through. Instead, when they ask me "What is it about?", I truthfully reply "They're expecting my call" and they put me through. I'm then greeted by someone who not only knows I am calling but who wants to hear from me and is interested in how I can help them.

---

[1] Market Transformations study, 2010.
[2] Random House Business, 2012.

The reason my calls are more productive is that they are preceded by a warm introduction, or 'referral'. Someone in my network, who ideally has a trusted relationship with my prospect, will have spoken to them in advance of my call. They have identified a problem my prospect has in their business, recommended me as a solution provider and arranged for me to make contact.

As a result, my prospect not only expects my call but knows that I can potentially make their life and job easier. In such circumstances, they tend to be more than happy to take the call and speak to me.

I should be preaching to the converted at this point. In my experience the majority of businesses recognise that referrals and recommendations are the best sources of qualified leads. Word of mouth introductions are more likely to convert into business than those from any other source.

In 2010 a study found that customers who came through referral spent more with a business, produced higher margins for that business in the early stages of their relationship, remained as customers of that business for a longer period of time and spent more with the business over time than customers who came through other routes to market.[3]

Unfortunately, while we may recognise the value of referrals, we don't necessarily put into place effective strategies to generate them. Many businesses will simply hope that their customers will refer them because they have done a good job. Others may ask for a few new names at the end of a sales meeting or include a footnote to their emails asking for recommendations. But that tends to be the extent of our activity.

In the meantime, we spend money on advertising, we devote resources to exhibiting at trade shows and . . .

. . . we pick up the phone and cold call.

---

[3] 'Referral Programs and Customer Value Schmitt', *Journal of Marketing*, July 2010, Philip Schmitt, Bernd Skiera and Christophe Van den Bulte.

A Referrals Strategy

There is another way. We can easily put into place a strong referrals strategy that is effective, easy to track and which costs very little in terms of time or money. Particularly once the foundations have been established.

In my book, *Recommended: How to Sell through Networking and Referrals*,[4] I outline how to put such a strategy into place. It's an approach based on understanding who your 'champions' are (the people who will refer you) and equally having a very clear vision of who your prospective customers (or 'prospects') are.

The approach I outline challenges you to understand who is ready to refer you, based on your relationship, the champions' understanding of your business and their opportunity to influence the right people. If you have done that groundwork and know who you want to meet, it should be fairly straightforward to get introduced to the people with whom you'd like to do business.

Of course, nothing in business is always straightforward and, like most business strategies, there are challenges and work involved. I'd love to say that I have a magic wand and you just have to wave it to get results, but we all know that if business was that easy we'd be discussing this on our yachts in the Caribbean.

There are two key challenges that my clients have to work through when implementing the referral strategy I share with them:

- time
- perception.

---

[4] Financial Times, Prentice Hall, 2011.

Any new approach to business takes time and effort to set up. A referrals strategy is no different. Time is required to identify your champions, and time is required to develop relationships with them so that they are happy and equipped to refer you.

The other challenge is more complicated. We are conditioned to look at our network in a particular way, giving labels to people we know based on our relationship with them. Hence we look at some people as family members, other as social contacts. Professionally (and we do like to distinguish between personal and professional networks), we label some as our clients, others as our suppliers, yet more as colleagues and then there are our competitors.

The nature of human interaction draws us to interact with each of these people in our network based on the label we have pinned on them and the groups we have consigned them to. We forget that they have a life beyond the life they have with us. We forget that they each have their own network of friends, family, suppliers, clients, colleagues and competitors.

And when we are looking for contacts we limit ourselves to the connections we see as a result of our relationship with them, ignoring the often vast diversity of contacts across the rest of their network.

The challenge for any business putting a referrals strategy in place is to put this limited perspective to one side. To recognise who can best introduce us to our prospects, we need to open the door to all of the combined networks of our champions, and we can't do that if we're governed by these traditional relationships.

But how do we get past this challenge? How can we find out to whom our connections are connected and where the best path to our prospects lies? And how can we do so without using up our scarcest resource – time?

Being Social

The answer lies in the brave new world of social networking sites and one in particular: LinkedIn.

They have become so all-consuming, it's easy to forget that we have only been using social networking sites for a relatively very short period of time; in many cases, only a few years. As I write this, I have windows open in my browsers for Facebook (two profiles, one personal and one professional), Twitter and LinkedIn. I'm always dipping in and out of one or another to post a thought, share a link or see what's happening elsewhere in my network.

In October 2011, social networking sites reached 82% of the global internet population and accounted for nearly one in every five minutes spent online. And, in case you thought that social networking was just for younger people, users aged over 55 represented the fastest growing age segment.[5]

While Facebook and Twitter, unlike LinkedIn, are perceived to be purely 'social', all three have, to differing degrees, professional uses. Of the three, LinkedIn is the one most commonly associated with, and used for, professional networking.

Effective Use of LinkedIn

Whenever I give presentations about LinkedIn, I ask participants two questions. To the first question – "How many of you are members of LinkedIn?" – in almost every audience the vast majority of hands shoot

---

[5] 'It's a Social World', Comscore, October 2011.

into the air. However, when I follow up by asking how many people use the site effectively, almost every hand disappears from view.

Professionals from all walks of life have now joined LinkedIn. In most cases, they post up brief details from their CV, accept connection requests from people they know – and then forget about the site.

The problem is that people join LinkedIn for the wrong reasons. They join because they have received several invitations, heard about it in the media or from colleagues, or because they fear redundancy. Little thought is given to how membership of the site will benefit them or what they need to do to get value from membership. They simply join because they feel they ought to.

Then day-to-day life gets in the way and they forget about it.

This is a common problem with much formal networking. We participate because we're invited, but don't have a clear objective or understanding of what's involved. With time a precious commodity, we then move on without ever engaging in a way that produces effective results.

But if we take the time to understand exactly how a network can help us, the potential is huge. Networks, whether formal sites and groups or simply the web of people to whom we are connected, offer us the opportunity to become better known, better equipped and better connected. They can help us to boost our profile in new markets; they can offer support and information; and they can help us find the introductions we need to potential customers.

LinkedIn offers all of these types of support, each one hugely valuable to any business. Yet most people don't know how to access that support and, as a result, their profile lies dormant on LinkedIn.

A simple understanding of how sites work and how they can produce the rewards above can make life so much easier for us, including getting referrals to key prospects so that we don't have to try to reach them through cold calls.

LinkedIn as a Referral Tool

To understand how to use LinkedIn as a referral tool, first of all we have to look at how it works. LinkedIn is structured on the principle of *six degrees of separation*, a theory that states we are no more than five steps from anyone in the world.[6] Before Reid Hoffman set up LinkedIn, he invested in the patent for this concept along with a colleague, Mark Pincus, with whom he invested in another social network, Friendster, and who went on to found yet another network, Tribe.

But for Hoffman, six degrees is three steps too far. He explains:

> *"Academically, the theory is correct, but when it comes to meeting people who can help you professionally, three degrees of separation is what matters. Three degrees is the magic number because when you're introduced to a second- or third-degree connection, at least one person in an introduction chain personally knows the origin or the target person."*[7]

Hoffman's point is that each person in a chain of three has a personal connection with either the person requesting the introduction or their prospect. And this is what makes it effective. "After all", he says, "why would a person bother to introduce a total stranger (even if that stranger is a friend of a friend of a friend) to another total stranger?"[8]

When you join LinkedIn you build your network by both requesting and accepting connections. The criteria by which you do this depend very much on what you want to achieve from membership. If, for example, you are purely using LinkedIn to generate trusted referrals, you should only connect to people who you'd be happy to refer and who, in turn, would be happy to refer you. If, however, you want to raise your profile in a particular market, you might choose to connect to influential individuals within that market.

---

[6] More information on six degrees of separation can be found in Chapter 8 of *Recommended: How to Sell through Networking and Referrals*.
[7] *The Start-Up of You* (Random House Business), 2012.
[8] *ibid.*

Once you are connected, you can then see who is, in turn, connected to the people within your network. These connections are your 'second degree network', in other words, you know people who know them.

If you have identified your 'champions', you can now use LinkedIn to research the introductions they could potentially make for you by exploring their networks.

People don't tend to respond to a general request for referrals (such as "If you know anyone who might benefit from my services . . . "). It leaves them with too much work to do. If you want people to refer you, it is important that you do the hard work for them and present them with a request for a *specific* introduction. Access to each of your champion's networks on LinkedIn helps you overcome the challenge of having to guess who they might know.

Allowing for the fact that not everyone has the strictest criteria for connections and some of your contacts may have connections they don't personally know, LinkedIn will still give you a good guide to referrals you can ask for.

Bypassing the Gatekeeper

A much more powerful approach is to target your prospects and use LinkedIn to find out how your network can connect you to them, bypassing the 'gatekeeper' in the process. While you can see your second degree network on LinkedIn by looking at your connections' connections, you can't directly see those people's connections (your third degree network).

However, what you can do is *search* for your prospects. LinkedIn has a very good advanced search engine that allows you to find people not only by name but by company, job title, location, industry and other options. If you upgrade there are even more criteria by which to filter your search.

The site will then tell you how you are connected to the people it finds for you. If they are a second degree connection, LinkedIn will tell you which connection you have in common.

If your prospect is a third degree connection, LinkedIn will tell you which of your contacts knows someone who knows your prospect. It won't tell you who the prospect's contact is, as you cannot directly see the networks of people to whom you're not directly connected, but it does let you see where the route lies and you are then able to ask your connection if they can facilitate an introduction.

There are people who argue that there is no need to go through this convoluted route. After all, if you sign up for a premium membership to LinkedIn , you can send 'Inmails' direct to prospects through the site.[9] However, people are more responsive to a request received through (and with the endorsement of) a trusted contact than they are to such unsolicited approaches.

Once you have identified your prospects and the connections that will lead you to them through the site, you can then request an introduction. You can do this through the site, sending a message to your prospect which you ask your connection to pass along for you. Alternatively, you can just pick up the phone or email your contact directly, having used LinkedIn purely for research.

Either approach can be effective. In December 2011 I was due to travel to Dublin to deliver some training and to meet with a couple of companies to whom I had been referred. With spare time on my hands I decided to look for other possible meetings, and used LinkedIn to search for connections.

---

[9] At the time of writing, everything outlined in this chapter can be accessed under the free Basic Membership on LinkedIn unless otherwise stated.

Using the advanced search facility on the site, I looked for sales directors in financial services based within 50 miles of Dublin. The site gave me the choice of 89 people who fitted my criteria and who were second degree contacts.

Two of them were a great fit as potential clients and had contacts I knew well. I sent a message introducing myself and requesting a meeting with both prospective clients through our mutual connections on the site. I also called each of my connections to let them know I had requested the introduction and asking if they would be happy to facilitate it.

In both cases the messages were passed on and the prospects responded to me positively.

Not everyone is a fan of the facility provided by LinkedIn to request introductions, however. In their book *How to Really Use LinkedIn*,[10] Jan Vermeiren and Bert Verdonck stress, "If you insist on using the 'Get Introduced Through' option you should know that both the person who introduces you as well as the one being introduced can read both messages! Most people are unaware of this and write something (too) personal in the message to the person who will introduce them."

Vermeiren and Verdonck offer an alternative they call the 'Magic Email'. Following a phone call, similar to the one I suggest above, they recommend sending an email to your contact requesting the introduction, in a format that can be forwarded and reframed by the sender.

"If you use the 'Get Introduced Through' option, YOU need to write a message that can be forwarded by your contact", they explain. "This is a cold message that is warmed up a bit by your contact. But it is still you, a stranger, who wrote the message.

---

[10] Networking Coach, second edition, 2011.

"On the other hand, when the person you want to reach on LinkedIn receives a message from a mutual contact, someone they already KNOW, LIKE and TRUST to a certain level, they will be much more open to the message. At the least, this person will be more open to a conversation with you; at best you are already 'presold' by your mutual contact!"[11]

Saving Time and Generating Results

Whichever path you choose, it doesn't take much time or effort to use LinkedIn to generate referrals. It may seem daunting at first to develop an effective profile, build a network and then ask for your first referral, but once the foundations are in place you can enjoy tremendous rewards for very little effort.

How much difference would it make to your business if you spent 30 minutes a day, or even a week, searching for prospects on LinkedIn and asking for introductions? If you have connected with the right people, those who know, like and trust you, how many qualified referrals could you enjoy as a result of that activity?

If the introductions have come through strong contacts who are happy to endorse you, what proportion of those referrals would you expect to convert? How much business could you make as a result of that half an hour's activity?

All without ever having to make a cold call again.

---

[11] *How to Really Use LinkedIn* (Networking Coach), second edition 2011.

TWITTER FOR BUSINESS

by Francesca James

About Francesca James

FRANCESCA JAMES is a journalist and blogger specialising in social media and technology for business. You can find her on Twitter @francescaajames.

A S OF SUMMER 2012, Twitter had 10 million active users in the UK and 140 million worldwide. Not bad for a network that was born in 2006. Since its launch, Twitter has occupied many a headline and become increasingly entwined with everyday life. It has been blamed for inciting riots and undermining super injunctions; and credited with accelerating a move to democracy across the Middle East.

Personally, I was a bit slow on the uptake with Twitter. Facebook was the only place I hung out online. I have to admit, I didn't 'get it' for a long time. I even had an account for a year that I tweeted from just once. Or maybe twice.

Then everything changed. After hearing more and more people singing its praises, I finally downloaded the Twitter app on my mobile phone. I sunk a week into it, and the breadth and speed of interactions hooked me. I haven't looked back since. Twitter is now my first port of call for news, information, help, advice and for seeking and sharing content. I even wrote a dissertation about it.

When I started running Fresh Business Thinking's social media strategy, Twitter, for me, was where it was at. Yes, we had a Facebook presence, LinkedIn groups and a YouTube channel. But Twitter offered something truly unique on top of these.

In this chapter I want to explain what that is, and show you how to get the most out of Twitter for your business. At Fresh Business Thinking I oversaw our Twitter following grow from 1,800 to around 13,000. I'm going to share with you some actionable tips that I learned along the way.

So How *Exactly* Can Twitter Help Your Business?

A well-thought-out Twitter strategy coupled with great profile management can:

- enhance brand exposure
- establish you as an authority in your field
- update your followers with company and industry news
- provide loyal followers with latest promotions and offers
- drive additional traffic to your website
- improve the number of conversions
- build long-lasting, valuable relationships
- create opportunities for media exposure.

Twitter jargon buster

You may already be familiar with Twitter. If so, that's great – there should be plenty in this chapter that's new to you and of use for your business. If you're not, don't worry! Here's a quick jargon buster that covers all the core elements (and quirks) of the platform. Skip if you're *au fait*; take a quick look if you're not:

Tweet – A *tweet* is any message that you send on Twitter. It can be up to 140 characters long. You can send public tweets (the most common sort), which are just typed into the compose box and appear on your Home feed and the feed of anyone following you. You can send public reply and retweets (hit the reply or retweet symbols on anyone else's tweet). These will appear in your Home feed, and in the Connect feed of whoever you retweet or reply to. Retweets also appear in your followers' Home feeds. Lastly, you can send direct messages to anyone who you're following who is also following you. No one else sees them.

Followers – These are other Twitter users who have chosen to subscribe to read your tweets. They see all public tweets and retweets you publish. Their tweets will not appear in your feed unless you are following them.

Handle – This is Twitter-speak for username. For example, mine is @francescaajames

@ – The @ symbol is used to mention and communicate with other Twitter users. For example, if you wanted to contact me or reply to me on Twitter you would have to include @francescaajames in your message. The same applies if you wanted to mention me and make sure I saw the tweet (even if it wasn't directly to me).

Bio – This is your 'about you' section on your profile. Twitter gives you 160 characters for this.

– This is a **hashtag**. Think of the hashtag as part of a cataloguing system. It helps people find things they're interested in in the vast pool that is Twitter. Placed before a word (or phrase), a hashtag allows users to click on the word and find all other Tweets that use it. You can also search for a given hashtag. So if I wanted to find out more about what is going on in my hometown of Cardiff I would search #Cardiff and any tweets containing #Cardiff would show up.

> **The Sprout** @FeedtheSprout
> Sunday = Ian McCulloch @Swnfestival #Cardiff ow.ly/cR3rK
> Expand
>
> **Breast Cancer Care** @BCCare
> We're just £65 from our fundraising total bcc.cx/QX9cNr Thanks for your support. Right now, @RachaelPower2 is cycling around #Cardiff
> View summary
>
> **Francesca James** @FrancescaaJames
> Making my small screen debut on @itvwales some time next week. Filming at the new @indycube location Castle arcade #Cardiff this morning
> Expand

If I wanted to be more specific and search for, say, jobs in Cardiff, I could search #Cardiffjobs or #JobsinCardiff. Note there are no spaces between words when using a hashtag. Hashtags are used frequently by Twitter users. Some are generic and hundreds of tweets swamp the search; others are more specific. We'll learn more about using hashtags effectively later.

#FF – This stands for Follow Friday. On Fridays people tweet #FF or #followfriday before a list of Twitter handles that they think other people should follow.

RT or Retweet – If you see a tweet you like, you might decide to share it with your followers. You can do this by pressing the retweet button in the top right of the tweet that's tickled you. The tweet is then rebroadcast to your followers whilst crediting the original poster.

Trending topic – If a word or phrase (or hashtag) is popular enough it will become a trending topic. You can see these on the lower left hand side of your dashboard. You can choose whether you want to see worldwide trending topics, countrywide or trending topics in specific parts of your country.

Tailored topic – Twitter has recently launched tailored topics. Essentially they are trending topics based on your location and who you follow on Twitter.

* * *

So, now we're armed with the essential Twitter terminology, how can small businesses harness the true potential of Twitter to ensure maximum returns?

1. Big is Not Always Beautiful

Big is not always beautiful when it comes to social networks. We constantly hear the media refer to the number of followers a celebrity or big brand has (I did it myself earlier in this chapter). But if you scratch the surface you'll see that many of these super-popular accounts have a wealth of 'followers' that are *bots*.

These bots are web robots or software applications that run automated tasks online. Some of those tasks included following Twitter users. Others include spamming them. Studies have even suggested that close to half of all Twitter followers are bots. Despite this, many businesses still measure the success of their social media marketing by the number of followers they have *without* any reference to the quality and sincerity of the followers.

Therefore, when using Twitter for your business be sure not to set basic follower targets as your chief key performance indicator (KPI). It is much better for your business to have a *steadily growing, organic follower-*

base that engages with you and shares your content. A large number of 'people' following you who couldn't give two hoots what you're saying is nothing to brag about.

How do you go about getting that kind of follower? These tips will show you.

2. Don't Buy Followers

A bit of a follow on from tip (1) here. There are lots of organisations out there that offer to get you thousands of followers quickly on Twitter. They can even promise ones that are relevant to your business.

It won't cost you as much as you might think. For as little as £400 you can quickly and effortlessly plump up your Twitter following to 20,000-plus. Spend a little more and you can have an army of followers to rival some celebrities. But is there any point?

No. There is no point.

10,000+ followers seems to be something of a holy grail among tweeters. Well, that figure, if largely comprised of engaged, enthusiastic followers is great. But you won't get that kind of follower this way. It's impossible.

The only way to inflate numbers this quickly is by scooping in a whole host of unengaged and over-saturated – or fictional – users.

Resist the temptation.

3. Stop and Listen

Twitter is an amazing tool for listening in on what's happening in real-time. That, in turn, is the beginning of effective engagement – and growing your audience the best way.

In order to manage this effectively I suggest you sign up to a social media management client such as TweetDeck (**www.tweetdeck.com**) or HootSuite (**www.hootsuite.com**). Both are free and work in web browsers as well as through dedicated apps for Mac, Windows, iPhone and Android.

HootSuite and TweetDeck allow you to arrange multiple feeds, schedule tweets, manage numerous accounts on one page and (perhaps most usefully) monitor streams of conversation on Twitter that are of interest to your business.

You do this by setting up powerful filters or search streams in these apps for terms related to your business or interests. As an online resource for entrepreneurs, Fresh Business Thinking wants to monitor all things small business. So we have search streams set up to catch uses of various terms like 'small business' (and #smallbusiness), 'business news' (and #businessnews), and 'SME' (#SME).

These keep us in the know when it comes to what's happening in our area, and what people are saying. It lets us find good things to share, interesting things to comment on, and so on.

Sometimes, your company might get mentioned with an incorrect Twitter handle or even without any handle at all. If this happens, you won't get a notification saying that you've been mentioned and you may never learn what was being said. Search streams also help solve this problem.

For example, our handle is @freshbusiness but we might get mentions as 'Fresh Business Thinking' or @freshbusinessthinking. We don't want to miss these mentions, so we've set up a stream to notify us when they happen.

HootSuite is our tool of choice for this (check out TweetDeck too). Here's how you do it in this app:

1. Click the **+ Add Stream** button

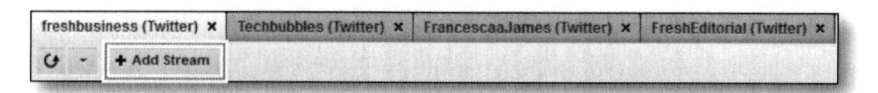

The +Add Stream button

The Add Stream window will then pop up. Stay on the default social network (which is Twitter). From here, click the **Keyword** tab.

The Keyword column

Add the keywords you'd like to track. When you're finished, click **Create Stream** on the bottom right of the window.

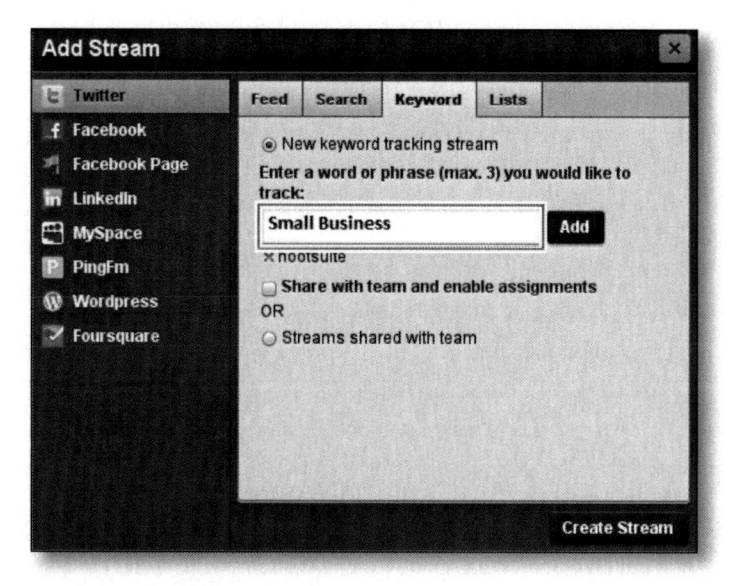

Filling in the keyword details

Before long, you'll see something that you can't stop yourself from commenting on. The engagement will be natural, rather than artificial – you interacting with people already discussing stuff you are both genuinely interested in. That's how you start attracting valuable followers.

4. Connect with Hashtags

Hashtags are a fantastic tool for businesses on Twitter.

Just to recap, hashtags catalogue tweets into areas of interest. For example, let's say you see the hashtag #smallbusiness. If you click on it you'll find all the most recent tweets using this hashtag. These are likely people interested in small business and people that we (Fresh Business Thinking) want to converse with.

So don't hold back from looking at hashtags relevant to your business and, where you have value to add, making contact with (or following) the people who have used them. And look for questions and problems that people have that you can solve. This is one big way you can use Twitter to establish your industry expertise and build your reputation.

If you want to measure the *popularity* of certain hashtags you can do so by using **www.hashtags.org**. This site gives you some (limited) free metrics. For example, you can use it to find out the number of tweets per hour for a given hashtag, the top users of a hashtag, as well as a hashtag's related hashtags. There is an option to upgrade to various paid tiered packages should you wish to extend your research.

This information could be useful to your business – it can allow you to join the right conversations. Below is an example of a graph delivered by **hashtags.org** showing the number of tweets each hour that use #smallbusiness in their tweets. This is useful to us. If someone is talking about #smallbusiness on Twitter, they'll probably like our site.

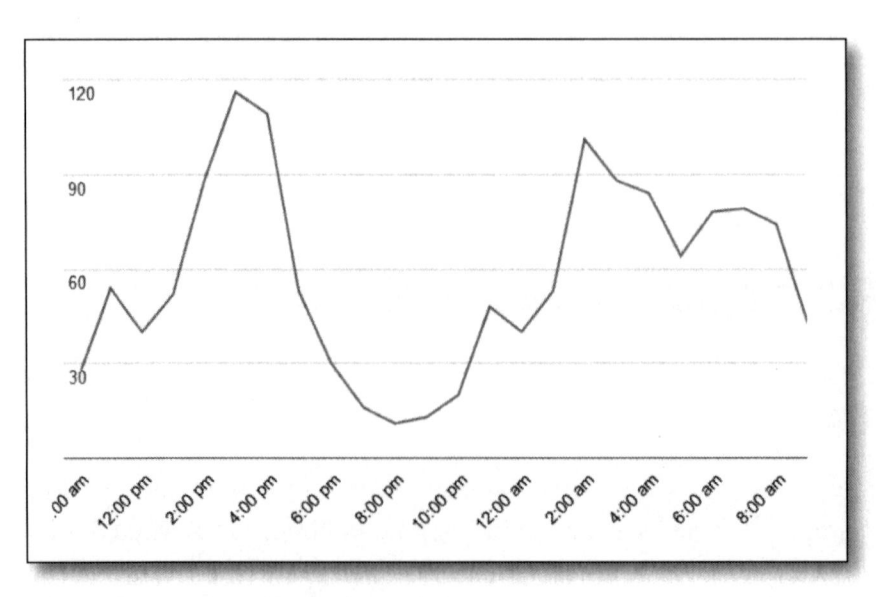

Talking about business (via hashtags.org)

5. Be Trendy with Hashtags

It's also worthwhile taking time to check trending hashtags and use any that are relevant to your areas of expertise. (Don't commit the Twitter sin of faking it, though, and adding an irrelevant hashtag to something else.)

You can piggyback on these hashtags by sharing content that relates to the topic alongside a repeat of the hashtag in your tweet. Remember that relevance is key as you do so.

Say you run a restaurant that's located next to a live music venue. If an artist playing there is trending on Twitter on the day of the concert, this might be an opportunity for you to promote yourselves to gig-goers as a friendly eatery perfect for pre- or post-gig food.

> *Excited that #RockStar will be playing just down the road in 2 hours. We've cooked extra noodles for all her fans – come by and sample!*

Television programmes are another good opportunity. Broadcasters are increasingly using Twitter to engage with their large audiences, with many programmes boasting official hashtags. (The same is also true of books and videogames.) By thinking outside the box, you can harness the potential of the large audiences for these media by commenting on story lines, characters or events in them that relate to your business.

There are plenty of TV shows that have direct or indirect links to businesses all over the world. Think *Great British Bake Off* if you're in catering or hospitality, *DIY SOS* if you renovate, build or plumb, or *Britain's Next Top Model* if you work in any part of the hair/beauty/fashion industries.

Just don't hijack a hashtag with irrelevant material.

6. Bad News: Deal With It

We live in an age where bad news travels like wildfire. For businesses, the biggest kind of bad news that Twitter can deliver is negative and very public feedback from a disgruntled customer.

The most important thing for your business is not to panic. Consider your reaction carefully. Even on a real-time network like Twitter, you have some time (although minutes rather than hours) before you need to respond. Do not post a knee-jerk reply. Unlike Facebook, Twitter doesn't allow you to delete other people's comments. And, although you can take down a tweet of your own, it's almost impossible to remove all record of it once it's gone out.

So before you do anything, assess the comments objectively. See if they have merit. If they do, thank the commenter for letting you know and tell them (if true) that you will be taking steps to remedy things. If possible, outline the steps you will be taking. At very least, let them know their complaint will be taken into consideration.

Consider whether you want your reply to go just to the user or to all your followers. Hitting reply and then just typing in your tweet after their handle will send your response directly to the user you're replying to, but not to your followers. (It'll still be publicly available if people click on your profile.) If an issue has bubbled over and you want all your followers to see your response, add something before the handle you're replying to (even just a full-stop or a quotemark). The reply tweet will then go to everyone following you.

> **@HypotheticalComplainer** *Sorry to hear about the issues you've been having. It should all be fixed now. Again, please accept our apologies.*

A reply that goes directly to one user

> .**@HypotheticalComplainer** *Sorry to hear about the issues you've been having. It should all be fixed now. Again, please accept our apologies.*

A reply that goes directly to all your followers

With a genuine complaint, once you have acknowledged on Twitter that it has been made, take the comment into a private channel – email or telephone – as soon as possible. If the comment is clearly unreasonable or ludicrous, the best option is to ignore it. Others viewing your Twitter feed are likely to do the same.

Negative comments are a part of the social landscape and the fact that you acknowledge them publicly shows that you are taking on customer feedback and seeking to continuously improve your service. You will not be seen as weak for responding to a negative comment – quite the opposite.

You will be surprised at how your influence grows if you are seen as open and honest about criticism.

7. Live Event Tweeting

Conferences and events are another good opportunity to make use of Twitter for your business. They provide heaps of shareable information that's great for Twitter – think stats, quotes, pictures.

Events usually have their own pre-assigned hashtag, too. If they don't, you can pick an obvious one for them.

Make sure anyone from your business attending an event uses the appropriate hashtag when tweeting about the event. This helps you get plugged into any other conversations going on about it.

8. Timing is Everything

It's all well and good setting aside an hour a day for tweeting. Unfortunately this can result in a very clumpy Twitter stream: silence all day, followed by a barrage of Tweets as soon as you get a spare hour, followed by more silence.

To combat this, you can use apps like those we met earlier: HootSuite and TweetDeck. These let you schedule tweets for publication throughout the day, week and/or month. They also have a new auto-scheduler function that will automatically schedule your content for optimum engagement.

9. Empower Your Ambassadors

Employees are your brand's greatest representatives. Sensible use of social media by employees can add substantial value to your marketing efforts.

The US-based company Zappos positively encourages staff to use Twitter. Around a third of its 1,500 employees are on the social network. When asked about their social media policy, Zappos founder Tony Hsieh said it simply reads: "Be real and use your best judgment".

It might sound a little scary to place your brand's online footprint in the hands of staff members. But aren't they the best placed to make sure that your customers have all of their questions answered quickly and politely?

Twitter provides a real opportunity for you to make the best use of their capabilities, and to become a more nimble and responsive business on the web.

10. Create Opportunities for Media Exposure

Being quoted or featured by a media publication, whether online or offline, is a great way to spread the word about your business. Many journalists, reporters and influential bloggers are very active on Twitter and use the network to research and crowd-source information for articles or posts they are writing.

Although a journalist might seek you out if you are particularly active and influential on Twitter, you can give yourself a better chance of getting some media exposure by looking out for their requests. A good way to do this is by using hashtags (yes, again!). There are a few hashtags that you should regularly have your eye on. Journalists will use hashtags like #journo #journorequest #HARO (Help a Reporter Out) to ask for quotes, help and case studies when researching a story.

If you're quick and have something interesting to say, they may very well use you as a source. If they do quote you, they will credit you/your business in the article. Online publications will also (usually) link to your website. This is a great way to position yourself as an industry expert and get your business in front of large audiences.

Final Thoughts

I hope these tips have offered you some new ideas and perhaps the confidence to give Twitter a serious go if you're yet to venture into the twittersphere.

To sum up this chapter in a nutshell: you and your business should be tweeting to create meaningful conversations that will ensure your brand sticks in the minds of your contacts and connections. If you do this well, someday, somewhere down the line, a potential customer will think of you rather than loading up Google to search.

Those who really 'get' Twitter for business know that it won't deliver *immediate* returns. But it can provide very good, long-term returns.

FACEBOOK MARKETING FOR SMALL BUSINESS

by Nichola Stott

About Nichola Stott

NICHOLA STOTT has over a decade of experience in online communications, and has worked for some of the worlds' largest digital communications businesses. On joining Yahoo! in 2005 as senior search business development manager, Nichola fell in love with search and social media – finding a natural aptitude for the business, and was soon promoted to head of UK commercial search partners; leaving in March 2009 to found theMediaFlow, an online marketing agency specialising in search and social media.

Following the launch of theMediaFlow in May 2009, Nichola quickly established a reputation as an industry- leading speaker and writer and is a regular contributor to SearchEngineWatch, SEO-Chicks, Econsultancy and State of Search. In 2012 theMediaFlow was awarded 'One-to-Watch' in the Wirehive 100 Digital Agency awards.

www.themediaflow.com

FACEBOOK IS THE world's largest and most frequently visited social network. In the United Kingdom there are more than 30 million Facebook users, a staggering 60% of the total UK online population. The largest age group is the 25–34 bracket (that's 7.7 million people), at 25% of UK users; though 60% of all users are aged 35 and over. The gender breakdown is pretty well equal: 52% female and 48% male.

With a broad user base like this it's almost certain that your existing and potential customers are already on Facebook. Marketing on Facebook gives you the opportunity to interact with these people in highly personal and engaging ways. It is, however, something of an art form.

Facebook users are there primarily to engage in *social* activities: communicating with friends, sharing funny or interesting stories and videos, playing games, organising activities. Although some direct commercial activities take place on Facebook, by far and away the most successful marketing on the platform is subtle, content-driven and with a strong emphasis on sharing. It requires creativity and planning.

In this chapter we're going to look at how to set up a Facebook page for your brand or business, and then explore some engaging content strategies for driving audience growth and participation.

Setting Up a Facebook Page

Facebook are keen on making sure that an individual's usage is authentic. Facebook accounts are for people and it is a violation of the terms of service (**www.facebook.com/legal/terms**) to create an account under a fake or a company name. Using Facebook as a business is perfectly possible – and very much encouraged – but to do so you'll need to create a *page* for your business. An individual must first have a genuine Facebook account of their own to do this (it's possible to do it without your own Facebook account, but you miss out on several key functions).

A business page is like a profile page for your business. Content you post to it appears in your timeline running down the centre of the page for all to see, as do interactions with users who have liked or commented on the page. (With a page, the main connection-mechanism occurs when a Facebook user decides to 'like' your page. This is different to individual accounts, where users send a friend request.)

As we'll see, the functionality afforded by a Facebook page is much more suitable for business marketing than an individual profile.

TIP

Don't worry if you want to remain anonymous on your business page. You can post content on a page as if from your company and without any mention of you. There's no need for your private profile to come into it, except behind the scenes. If you want to imbue your posts with the personality of those behind the business, though, you can also post from personal accounts that have been linked to the page.

Getting started

First, head to **www.facebook.com/page**

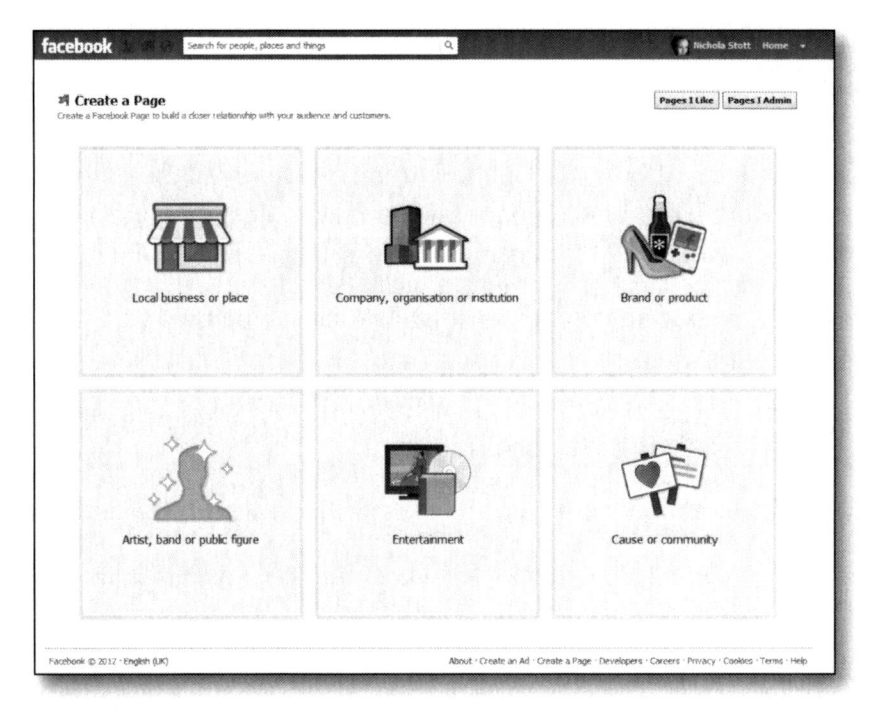

Create a page

This brings up the options for creating a page. Choose the type of business that best matches yours, and then a category within this. Don't worry if there's nothing that matches exactly. Just choose the closest for now. You can customise it further in advanced options once it's all set up.

For most small businesses the first choice – **Local business or place** – is probably most suitable, and I'll build the rest of the example around it. The process only varies very slightly between the business types.

Selecting the right type of page for your business is important as you will find that information fields available for you to fill out will cater to your choice. If, for example, you are promoting a book, creating a page for a book will reveal information fields that are expressly relevant to books (e.g. your ISBN number).

Claiming a place

A business 'place' may already exist for your business if another Facebook user has checked into your business location on their mobile Facebook app. This creates a page automatically, albeit not one under your control. You need to merge it with your page. Here's how . . .

First claim the unwanted page as an official representative:

- on the uncontrolled page click on
- select **Is this your business?**
- verify the additional information such as physical and web address
- claim the page, verifying your connection to the business either by email or by providing official documentation.

Now that you have claimed your page, go to the page that you want to keep:

- select **Update Info**
- then **Resources** on the lefthand menu

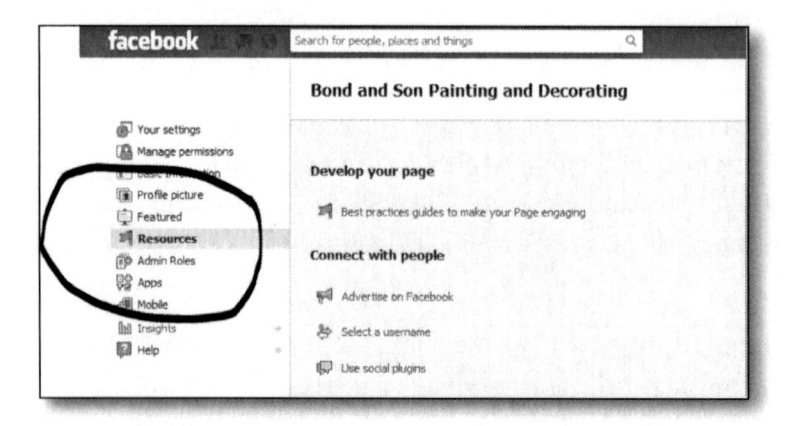

Resources

98 | HIT ME!

- click **Merge Duplicate Pages**.

Merging will take all the activity such as likes and check-ins from the other page; however, any content posted there (such as photos and status updates) will be lost.

Setting up a local business or place page

Click on the box **Local business or place**. Fill in the basic page details in the boxes shown.

Basic page details

In the second box (business name) be sure to enter the business name exactly as it is written and spelled in all other marketing material. This will reinforce brand recognition and help existing fans find you. The only exception is special characters such as '&'. **These should be written out.** You do not *have* to write them out, but as they are not permitted in the page URL it will help keep things clear for people if you do.

Once you have read and clicked the check-box to acknowledge the page terms (**www.facebook.com/page_guidelines.php**), click the **Get started** button.

> **TIP**
>
> Facebook frequently updates page terms and guidelines as well as related terms and usage policies without proactively notifying users. You are advised to regularly check the various terms; if you fail to comply with them, Facebook may revoke your page, meaning a loss of time and investment.

The next stage is to select your profile picture, often a company logo. Choose a square image. The image you upload must be 180 x 180 pixels at minimum; the final image, whatever you upload, will display at 160x160 pixels on your page (and a thumbnail of 32x32 in ads or newsfeeds: so make sure it scales!). If your image is a little more rectangular you will be given the opportunity to crop it during the upload process.

Profile picture

If you don't have a logo saved on the computer you're working on, Facebook can grab it from your site if you select **Import from website** here.

Set-up page

Next, fill in the details about your local business, providing as much detail as possible. Potential customers will rely on this information. Make it snappy and focused, but don't leave anything important out.

Here you also have the opportunity to add the URL of your website and other relevant URLs (e.g. your Google+ or YouTube page addresses).

Next, it's time to choose your Facebook web address (this is one of the things you can't do if you don't have an individual Facebook account). This is a short Facebook URL you can use throughout the rest of your online and offline marketing – e.g. in the footer of your website, or on business cards and compliment slips.

The default suggestion will be the same as your page name selected in the first step (if it's available). Unless your business name is extremely long and cumbersome it is best to retain the default web address here.

Once you have chosen your Facebook web address *it can't be changed*. Be sure you've checked its spelling and format with key business

> **Set up Bond and Son Painting and Decorating**
>
> 1 Profile picture 2 About **3 Facebook web address**
>
> Choose a unique Facebook web address to make it easier for people to find your Page. We've made a suggestion below, but you can also choose your own. Once this is set, it can't be changed.
>
> http://www.facebook.com/ BondAndSonPaintingAndDe
>
> **Set Address** Skip

Facebook web address

Once you click on **Set Address** the basic set-up of your Page is complete. You will then be taken to the page with the admin panel open. Facebook will suggest some set-up activities to get you started on the path to raising awareness of the page. These include the following:

- **Like:** if you 'like' a page this provides a connection between your business and the page in question. Those who have liked you can in turn see who your business has liked; it may appear as a story in their newsfeed, and it will also be viewable on your page.

- **Invite Friends:** prompts you to invite people from within your list of Facebook friends to like the page.

- **Email contacts:** as a business you may have a number of suppliers, customers and other business contacts that you connect to by email but may not be friends with on Facebook. This function allows you to email those contacts, inviting them to like the page, without you having to befriend them first. This is an example of where the page functionality is more suited to business than an individual account.

- **Share something:** such as a status update, a picture, link or video. This is the heart of running a good page on Facebook. It's content that, when posted, appears on your page's timeline, running down the centre of the page when people visit it. This content may also appear in your fans' newsfeeds. Sharing content about you, your business, things you are involved in, projects you've completed, other content that you like is the very stuff of Facebook. The more content you post and the more interesting and engaging that content, the greater the chance for audience growth in the form of new likes and re-shares of your content amongst your audience.

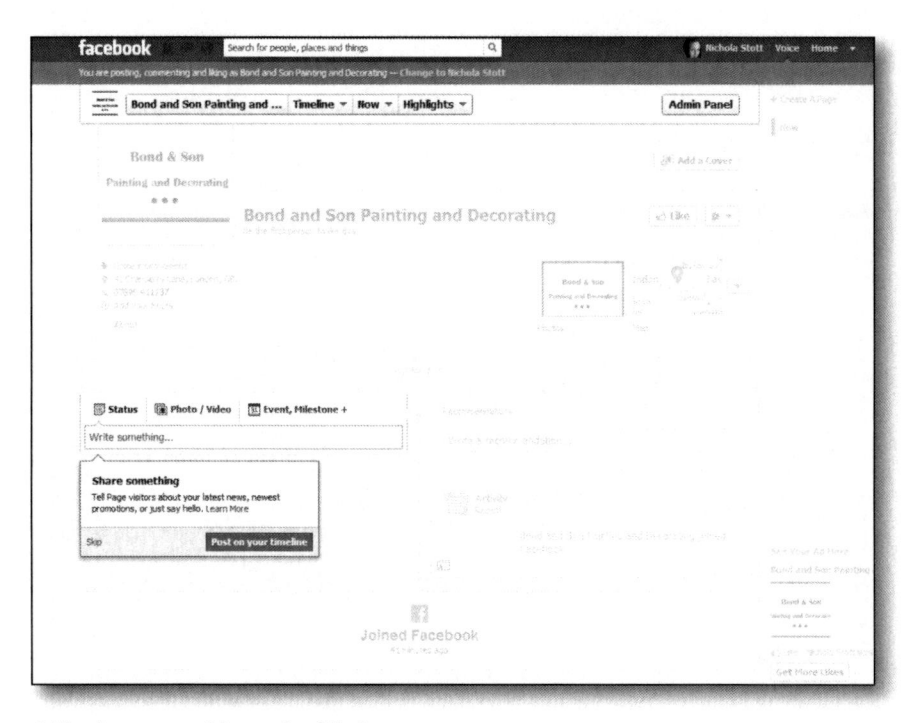

A blank page, waiting to be filled

Choosing a cover

Let's complete our page set-up. Your cover image sits behind your profile picture as a kind of widescreen background to the top of the page. It allows you to set the tone for your page. And it's a great chance to catch browsers' eyes. Don't be afraid to change it to keep it fresh.

Your cover image can be any image for which no other person or organisation holds rights: a photo display of your products, a snap from a recent event, or maybe some suitable stock imagery. It needs to be attractive and say something about your business. Optimal dimensions are 851 pixels wide by 315 pixels in height. As with a profile picture, you will be able to crop the image you upload if it does not scale to these landscape dimensions. But something hi-res and good quality, tailored for that space in advance, is strongly advised. For our example I have chosen an image from the Flickr Creative Commons (**www.flickr.com/creativecommons**), an online bank of photos with no known copyright restrictions.

Cover image

You now have the basics of your Facebook page in place. It's ready for use in your online marketing strategy.

One last thing before we move on. Do you see the message at the top of the page: "You are posting, commenting and liking as Bond and

Son Painting and Decorating" and the hyperlinked text **Change to Nichola Stott**? As mentioned earlier, you can use Facebook as your business or as yourself. Here's where you switch between the two identities. For the moment, anything I post will be done under my business name, but if I want to do something on the page and put a real name to it I can quickly switch over to my individual account.

How Does Facebook Marketing Work for Business?

Set measurable goals

Facebook is awash with 'unliked' and long-abandoned business pages. Few businesses realistically ask themselves what they hope to get out of Facebook and how to measure that. Without a sense of direction or progress – or even of what is possible in the first place – a half-hearted strategy is abandoned before really having had the chance to take seed.

Whilst Facebook may not be the best direct commerce channel for many businesses (in other words, it's not trying to be an eBay, Amazon Marketplace, or online storefront – at least not yet), it's an incredibly diverse and powerful tool for other things. This includes indirect marketing, information gathering, deepening relationships with existing customers and forging relationships with potential customers.

So the first thing to do is to set measurable goals. Getting to grips with 'engagement' metrics may seem unusual at first. It's not quite the same as the bottom line. But it's almost as vital – and in the long run it can't be separated from it.

By *engagement metrics* online marketers mean the data that shows an individual has interacted with your content in a way that demonstrates interest.

What to measure?

Within your page admin features, providing you have 50 or more likes, you will have access to **Insights for your Page**, where you can view interaction and engagement metrics – and, most importantly, the potential reach of your content.

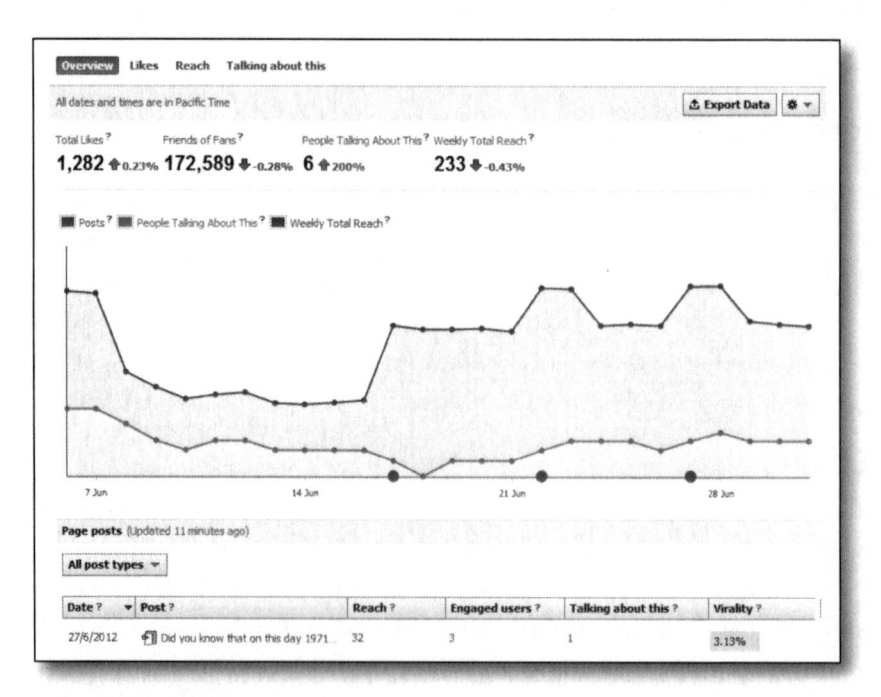

Insights for your Page

- **Total Likes:** the number of people who currently like your page.
- **Friends of Fans:** the total number of friends of those who like your page, giving you an indication of your page's potential reach.

- **People Talking About This:** the number of people who have created some kind of story about your page in the most recent week to-date, either by liking the page, contributing to your timeline (e.g. with a comment), liking a status message you have shared, or some other interaction with your content.
- **Weekly Total Reach:** the number of people who have seen any content associated with your page, posted by you or as a result of an interaction with that content from another Facebook user.

All of the above are calculated on a unique user basis.

> **TIP**
> If you have a website and use an analytics package to monitor your online traffic (such as Google Analytics) it is important to check how much referral traffic you get as a result of your efforts on Facebook.

Looking at these metrics, we can see that it is the *sharing* mechanisms of Facebook that bring your page to the attention of others. Therefore an interesting, consistent and engaging presence is the key to growing your presence on Facebook. You want to photograph, write about, videotape and pass on stuff that people will *want to share*.

Let's get into the ins and outs of that now.

Your Facebook Marketing Strategy

So now you have the page set up and know what to look for and measure when the likes start coming in. The difficult part is creating a content and communications strategy that delivers on your objectives.

Increasing your connections

As we have already discussed, it is unlikely for most local or small businesses that Facebook will generate many *direct* sales for you straight from your page (though there are ways, and we'll get onto those later). But Facebook is invaluable in raising brand awareness, encouraging interaction with and attachment to your brand, particularly through exclusive and time-sensitive content. And this, of course, boosts sales in the long run.

Here are some pointers on how to increase your Facebook connections:

- **Vary the style of post:** use pictures, video, polls and links as well as text. Upload photos of your latest and greatest creation before you post it out, ask for video testimonials from customers or show people around your workspace.

- **Share content from other sources.** This is social media, after all! It's a generous way of making yourself known to those who might be able to help you reach their customers in future with a similar 'like' or re-post.

- **Respond to all reader comments and suggestions:** both in the comments sections and by taking inspiration from them for new posts (where suitable) too.

- **Post offers to generate revenue and buzz:** click offers in the composer box, enter the details and T&Cs, and then sit back and watch customers snap it up and have Facebook tell their friends about it (it can appear in their newsfeed).

- Similarly, reward your fans and bring in new ones by using **whisper codes**: word-of-mouth vouchers you post as a status update that, when mentioned in an email or your real-world shop, entitle customers to a giveaway or other goodie. Cupcakery to the stars – Sprinkles of Beverley Hills – has famously used these to tremendous effect. They're brilliantly shareable.

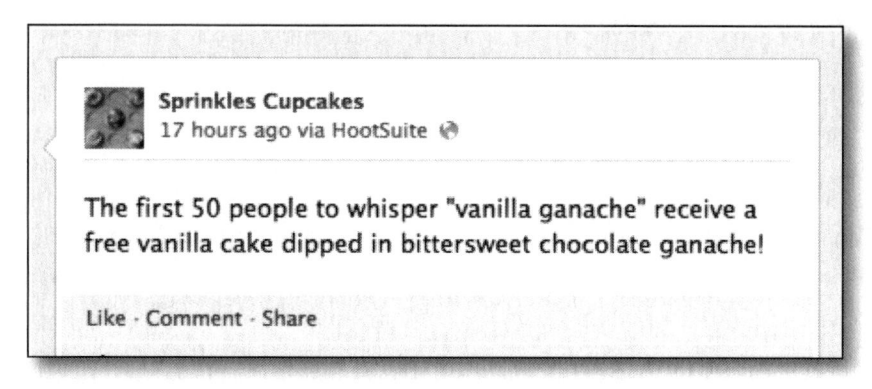

> **Sprinkles Cupcakes**
> 17 hours ago via HootSuite
>
> The first 50 people to whisper "vanilla ganache" receive a free vanilla cake dipped in bittersweet chocolate ganache!
>
> Like · Comment · Share

A whisper code in action

- Make sure you **include your page URL on your marketing materials**: both online and in the real world. Pub mirrors have started cropping up with them on. So have restaurant menus. Think about where you could share yours.

- Likewise, if you have a real-world storefront **use point-of-sale signage** to encourage visitors to 'check in' to your Facebook place on their smartphones when visiting.

Content style

- **Images** (in a style that is in-keeping with your brand) are more likely to be shared than other types of content such as text or video.

- Posting **questions** or making use of the poll feature will provoke more responses and interaction than statements.

- **Posting updates directly** from Facebook, as opposed to using Twitter, LinkedIn or auto-posting software to 'scattergun' posts, leads to higher rates of engagement (presumably as people know that you are 'there').

Content strategy

The key to successful Facebook business content is engaging and interesting material combined with patience and persistence. Planning out well-balanced, regular updates in advance is vital.

Build an editorial calendar which splits the week up into different kinds of content each day to give you regular, varied updates. For example:

- 'What's happening this week?' (Sunday)
- 'Weekly giveaway' (Monday)
- 'Featured event' (Tuesday)
- 'Creator spotlight' (Wednesday)
- 'Today in [insert industry]' (Thursday)
- 'Sneak peak' (Friday)
- 'Trivia' (Saturday).

Add significant events to your editorial calendar and build round them. Be aware of cultural and national events (and sensitivities).

Content ideas

Content ideas can be the most difficult thing to come up with, particularly if you are new to social media or not a natural 'sharer'. To get your creative juices flowing I've created a few example scenarios which may spark similar ideas for your business.

1. *"I'm a glass blower. I make beautiful decorative pieces for consumers and businesses. How do I promote my content to both audiences without alienating one or the other?"*

A Facebook page for any business that creates visually appealing products – be it fashion, design or art – must make use of the ability to create, upload and manage photos. In this case I'd recommend creating albums that cut across, as well as reflect different client groups. For example, have an album to store photos of all vases, and an album for both private and corporate commissions. Images can then appear in multiple locations. In addition you can encourage people to post pictures of their products in-situ in their home or office.

When taking photos, don't be afraid to share the inner-workings of your business as opposed to finished products. In fact, seeing the ins and outs of production is much more interesting and shareable than pristine photos of final products.

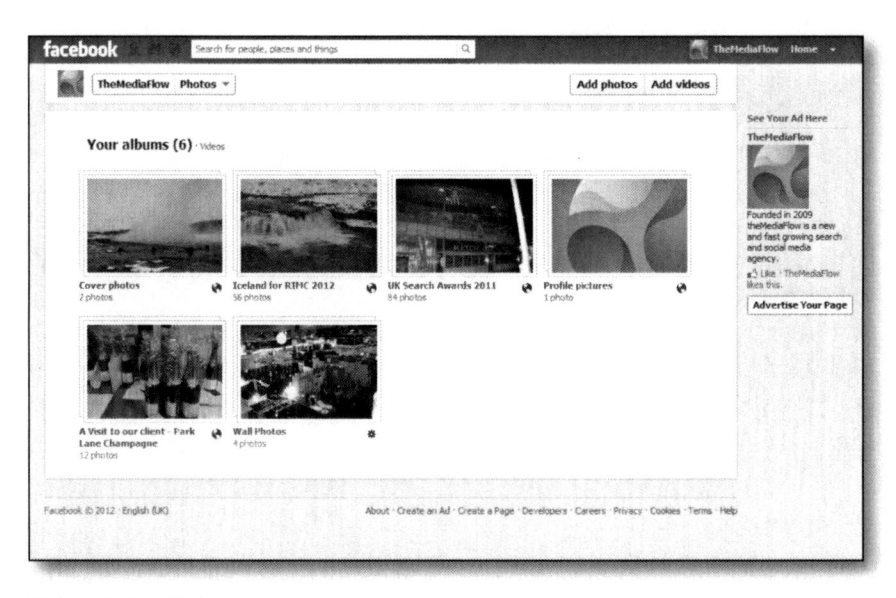

Using photo albums

2. *"We make tool belts which are used by plumbers, carpenters and the like who need both hands to work, and quick access to their tools. The product is hardly glamorous or social and as it's so hardwearing most customers will buy only two or three in their life."*

If your product is a 'lifetime' product that means it's almost certainly going to be able to rely on a reputation and some form of emotional attachment with your customers. After all, it'll be around with them for a long time. The best approach is to build on this foundation to become a brand synonymous with the product-type in the same way that people will describe any digger as a JCB, or any adhesive tape as Sellotape.

Even if a product isn't particularly glamorous, there can be good opportunities for some tongue-in-cheek fun. I'd suggest running competitions and offers for existing customers, encouraging them to post pictures of themselves wearing their tool-belts on your page. As an additional incentive you could offer a monthly prize of £50 vouchers to the best customised tool-belt.

For the competition title, how about 'The Biggest Tool'?

3. *"I'm a franchise-owner locksmith, one of many operating across my county. How can I distinguish myself when we all offer the exact same service?"*

This is where ingenuity and being first in your social marketing strategy will help.

Getting customer reviews or permission to reference a testimonial can be quite difficult, but it's a good focus to have for your Facebook page in this kind of business. Fortunately, people will often be grateful when you help them in your business, since you specialise in solving inconveniences.

Whatever your business, focus on what customers get out of it, and use that to determine your approach to Facebook. Facebook is all about interacting authentically with your customers. Meet them where they meet you.

So as soon as you finish a job at your locksmith's, why not post a status update on your Facebook page, e.g.

> *"Just got Julie and her three hungry kids into the house in twenty minutes after an accidental school-run, with the keys locked in the house!"*

> *"Trevor was so grateful I managed to get him into the house at 1.00am after his night out, that he insisted I share his pizza!"*

Just be careful to protect a customer's privacy and security whatever your business. Fail to do that and it will backfire.

Selling on Facebook

You can use a Facebook app to create a store within your business page if you want. If your product is right for it, this can be a very neat way of simplifying sales conversion, though be careful about scaring others away by being too commercial.

Store apps include:

- **www.facebook.com/aradium**
- **www.facebook.com/moonfruit**
- **www.facebook.com/ondango**
- **www.facebook.com/vendiostores**
- **apps.facebook.com/vendorshop**

There's no store app developed by Facebook (as yet), and each of the above has different terms. Check them out thoroughly before signing up to make sure they're right for you.

A Note on Facebook Ads and Sponsored Stories

Whilst this chapter examines the marketing opportunities available on Facebook, there are additional advertising and paid-for promotional opportunities with ads and sponsored stories.

Ads can be used to drive users to your page or to an external site. Sponsored stories point to your page.

Ads can be targeted with incredible precision, taking in location, age, sex, interests, connections, relationships, languages, education and career. You can also reach users based on their interests and the information they've provided in their timeline. Sponsored stories appear for users whose friends have interacted with your page in some way.

Check out the official guide to Facebook ads and sponsored stories at **fbrep.com//SMB/Ads_Create_Flow.pdf**.

Get Started!

Facebook is *the* social media giant and marketing on Facebook is a powerful and unparalleled resource. Best of all, every single one of its core features is free – only advertising costs you anything. All it requires is thought and time. Armed with this chapter, you should have everything you need to get your business onto it in style. 850 million users just got one giant step closer. Good luck!

WINNING CUSTOMERS WITH REPORTS

by David White

About David White

DAVID WHITE formed **Weboptimiser.com** in 1996 with the strange idea that selling services to pioneers would work. It did, and continues to today. Since then he has worked for banks; stallholders; B2B and B2C companies; very large brands; one-man bands; rock'n'rollers; translators – locally, nationally and globally.

He defined best practice when he chaired the IAB Search Council and has delivered SEO, pay-per-click and social media services with huge returns on investment to a range of clients.

David is available for keynote presentations and has co-authored four books. Others are in the 'works'.

The ideas and concepts mentioned in this chapter can be seen in action at **Weboptimiser.com** and **TribalIdeas.com**.

I HAVE BEEN working in online marketing for a long time. I was even lucky enough to have a hand in naming the practice of 'web optimising' and SEO with my first sites, **weboptimiser.com** (and **weboptimizer.com**) in 1996.

But my industry could not be more competitive. Since 1996, countless competitors have arrived and disappeared. Other companies have brought web optimising in-house. Many of my competitors are gargantuan: Google now has staff called 'web optimizers'.

How have we survived? How have we consistently found (and won) new customers?

The answer is simple on the surface, but I think it's pretty profound underneath. We really value our customers. We don't just love them. We're not just really glad they exist. (Though existing is pretty important, of course.) We take an interest in them as people. All our marketing grows out of that interest.

The best companies and individuals that I have worked with have taken the same approach. It's not enough to have a target market. You have to know that market inside out; and you have to be able to help them before they even become a customer.

In my experience, the most effective online marketing medium for this is a website with enticing content, coupled with a regular report that offers much more. When this chapter is over I hope you'll see how, unlike any other marketing method, it allows you to start, build and profit from genuine relationships with good customers.

* * *

So in the rest of this chapter I'm going to walk you through the process that I employ with an extended example. I have created a simple website called Tribal Ideas, found at **TribalIdeas.com**. I have added some content to it and placed an offer for a free report on it. These are my basic building blocks for a customer-centric marketing approach.

The seven tactics that follow explain the ins and outs of what you do next.

1. Make it Optional

When people accept your report let them know that, as soon as they are ready, you have even more in store for them. But tell them that they'll have to opt-in to receive it.

Why?

Their initial subscription to your report may just have been out of idle curiosity, perhaps out of politeness. And that's not enough to allow you to keep in contact with them and get anything out of the relationship. You're looking for something longer term than adding their name to a database and firing off instantly deleted spam once a month.

This process is all about *engaging*. One thing we all want to do in business is to engage with potential clients who show interest. By giving them the option of receiving more content after they've tried (and liked) the first sample, you're treating them right, and making sure that future contact will be worth it.

2. Help Them First

In my example over at **Tribalideas.com** I have prepared six reports in total. Each report contains real value, some of my best ideas and most interesting research. It's important that your reports feature good content like this. You don't need to give away everything you know, or all that your business can provide. But you won't get away with a lack of substance. Teasing people doesn't turn them into customers.

The reports also contain a number of key elements, including a case study and practical methodologies. They're sprinkled with humour. Your reports must be designed to show you as a real, genuine, friendly and capable person – those are the attributes that someone needs to see and experience before they buy from you.

3. Multiply to Identify

Having *multiple* reports allows you to identify your prospects' priorities. Giving them a choice of reports to download will quickly tell you what they are interested in. It's also made your business helpful to them already: you've met them where their needs or interests are, not just sent off what you think they should want to know.

Reciprocity plays a key part in sales psychology: customers respond positively to businesses that help them before they're customers. In other words, the more you give, the more you will get back. A little bit of trust, built through delivering results in advance, goes a long way.

So, so far, the report method has enabled you to find out a customer's prospective needs first and shown them how you can help. A much better position to be in than standing around shouting from the sidelines, don't you think?

4. Keep it Real

If you look at each of my reports, they consist of about 20% core content and 80% human interest. If I was really hard on myself I could reduce each report to maybe three paragraphs. Just the bare bones: jumping right away to the key elements and conclusion.

But experience shows that isn't enough to satisfy most people. Shorn of detail and relatable content, the best advice in the world can look unoriginal, copy-and-pasted and obvious.

The addition of personal information and commentary makes your work more authentic. And that makes it more effective. Thomas Power, founder of **Ecademy.com**, says that the key to social media is being yourself and building a brand around who you are. It's not about what you do – or, at least it's not about *what* you do in any way that is separated from *who* you are.

Making your reports personable not only gives your advice the best chance to shine, it also builds relationships with your potential customers. Business isn't conducted between robots. It's personal. Call it insurance, if you will: buyers need to feel comfortable with who they are buying from and they will pay a premium for this.

Making your content inescapably *you* is the answer.

5. Use Different Media

It's important to mix things up by using different media. Make a point of providing something by post – a free Christmas present; a special annual round-up – or have some reports delivered as online videos. Podcasts are good, too.

This keeps things fresh and memorable. It also means you don't miss out on people who strongly prefer one medium to another.

6. The Call to Action (I)

Now that readers can see you are willing and able to share good information – and hopefully like your style and personality too – you're in a position to make small offers of direct help.

The nature of the offers will obviously depend on your business and expertise. It may be that you can write a small report on a particular topic if requested. It may be that a personal call with you could be useful to them. It may be that you have a live event coming up and you can offer them a ticket.

Things like this can be made available to your readers for free or for a small charge: the goal at this stage is not to make money so much as to consolidate the reciprocity you've been building up. By bringing the fruitful relationship into the real world, and personalising it, you're getting close to making new, profitable, long-term customers.

7. The Call to Action (II)

So you've supplied information to potential customers, cultivated a more qualified list of interested contacts, given these contacts further useful information, and developed the relationships through personalised offers. The relationships are now mature. You have proven your consistency. You are the expert; the 'go-to' guy or gal.

Now it's only a matter of time until your contacts ask you for a quote or recommend you to others. You can also begin to pitch to them. The key is to be specific and targeted, and to begin with an opportunity, flag the problems that lie in the way, and present your services as the solution. Match it with an offer. Consider direct as well as affiliate sales; if you know another business that is right for them, you can point them in that direction without loss.

Final Thoughts

Of course, some of those interested in your site and reports may well be your competitors. That is a fact of life and not one that's worth worrying about. Remember that 80:20 rule? 80% of your reports should consist of your personality and experience, friendly case studies and reflections. Only 20% should be really detailed content. That means that, as most of your content is personalised, it is going to be very difficult to copy without your competitors looking like you. And they won't want that.

You will notice that I have identified seven strategies in this chapter. A number like seven is a good way of organising your content: lists, particularly of neat numbers like three, or seven, or ten always prove popular online. Being specific in advance helps people know what they're getting into and promises specific bits of meat on the bone: much more alluring than general promises of 'advice'.

I hope the seven tactics here have been worth your while.

THE ART OF WEB DESIGN

by Malcolm Graham

About Malcolm Graham

MALCOLM GRAHAM has advised some of the world's leading organisations on digital marketing strategy including the *Financial Times*, BP and the British Army. Malcolm is currently the CEO of LimeTree (**www.limetreeonline.com**), a rapidly expanding digital marketing agency based in London. Malcolm lives with his wife and son in London. His Twitter handle is @malcolmcgraham.

I DESIGNED MY first website in 1994: an advertisement for a holiday cottage in Pembrokeshire. Since then, I have worked on some of the most famous websites in the world and designed hundreds more for small to medium-sized companies.

Even though a lot has changed in the last 18 years, many of those same principles that I picked up when I was first starting out still serve me well. In this chapter, I want to share some of them with you. You don't have to be designing your site yourself; they should also be helpful if you're simply overseeing someone you've commissioned to design a site for you.

In many ways, web design is like designing a sports car: the product must look impressive but it also has to serve a purpose and get the user to a destination. It is neither pure design nor pure engineering. The skills of both a designer and an engineer are required to make a good website – and if you ignore one half of the equation you are destined to fail.

The web today

Here are perhaps the most important aspects of today's online world:

1. Mobile

2. Google

3. Social media (Twitter, Facebook and LinkedIn)

4. Video (YouTube)

5. HTML5

Mobile

Today, it is estimated that around 15% of all web traffic comes from mobile devices. Moreover, around 50% of traffic on social media and from email marketing is now via mobile devices.

Google

Google is the most important brand name on the internet. Indeed, no public-facing website can be built (at least, in the English speaking world) without first answering the following question: how will this site perform on Google?

Social media

During the early days of web design, there was no 'real' social media. Of course, there were bulletin boards, instant messengers and so forth – though these were typically closed or hard-to-find networks.

Video

Although it is hard to conceive now, when I first started work as a web designer video was just not possible. Everyone was using the internet via dial-up connections or slow university networks, so video streaming seemed an altogether distant prospect. Now, in 2012, video makes up a key component of most digital marketing strategies.

HTML5

Finally, HTML 5 is giving designers more flexibility in how they choose to go about creating their sites. It gives them the option to use a much wider variety of fonts, for example. With HTML 5, it is also possible to create much richer user experiences. It isn't perfect, however, and there are a significant amount of users with browsers that do not support HTML 5.

* * *

The internet is the one must-have piece of media that every business needs. You cannot (or at least should not) expect to launch a company without first having an internet strategy. Most of my start-up clients will register a domain name before they register their company. Many clients even launch a website before starting to trade. That's not all you need to do, though. Many business websites today add no value and can even damage the prospects of new companies.

So how do you get it right?

Key Metrics

Here are the key metrics that you need to understand in order to measure how your website is performing:

1. CPA – This stands for *cost per acquisition*. This is the cost for signing up a new customer.

2. CPL – This stands for *cost per lead*. This is the cost of generating a sales lead.

3. Bounce rate – The amount of people that bounce off a page without performing any action. Ideally, this should be 30% or less.

4. Average time on site – Poor, 'spammy' websites almost always have a low average time on site. You should aim to have an average time on site of at least four or five minutes.

5. Average number of pages visited – If your site has a lot of content then this statistic is also important. Typically, a good average for the amount of pages visited per user would be about ten.

If you can understand these metrics, you will be better equipped to measure the performance of your site.

User-testing

However, even with the stats above, every site should also be put through a professional user-testing programme. I would recommend using an online service, rather than setting up a usability lab, as it is more likely that you will get an honest, natural response. Online user-testing services are also much cheaper than setting up a lab and getting everyone to travel there.

User-testing will provide you with detailed feedback on your website which can be used in the design process. Remember, a website is different from other forms of media. It should continually evolve over time. It should never be 'finished'.

So those are the key metrics – and once you have good scores, your website will be successful.

Getting Good Scores

How do you get good scores? First, make sure you choose a good web designer. Be sure to avoid automated cheap online services – the end result will not look unique or distinctive and you'll have problems when you need to make changes or updates. Ultimately, if your site looks cheap then it will put people off.

Another major problem with finding high quality web design is that there are many people out there who will offer you a bespoke website for some ridiculous price, like £9.99. Let me tell you now – you cannot get a good, bespoke website made for £9.99, or even £99.99. In fact, £999 as a budget would only suffice for the most basic of websites. Bear in mind that even a simple web design can take over 30 hours to build. Good web designers who have experience and the right technical skills are not going to work for peanuts. And if you do decide to pay peanuts, you'll get monkeys. If you are restricted to a very small budget, then just ask for something simple.

It is also a fact that many web design projects do not get completed. Often, the client will pay some sort of deposit and then the designer will not deliver. There are various problems on both sides of the process that can cause this to occur. One such problem is often referred to as scope creep. This is when a client keeps changing their requirements, but not their budget, and the project becomes unsustainable. If the web designer has under-quoted just to win the business, often the project will not be completed or it will be of poor quality. Therefore, it is partly your responsibility as a client to provide a reasonable budget for the project. However, it is also the responsibility of the web designer to quote realistically. That is not to say that sometimes a smart web designer won't do a 'loss leader' project to crack a new high profile client account. That is just good business.

Apart from that, you should also ensure that you have a good working relationship with the web designer or firm. If you opt to use an agency, then be sure to hold a call or a meeting with the key people there – it is important that they prove to be professional and that you think you will get on with them.

In my own personal experience, people with some background in IT tend to deliver web design projects better. If their background is in design or marketing, then they may well struggle with some of the key technical detail. This is not to say that design and marketing skills are not vital. However, the internet was originally the domain of the computer enthusiast and some things will always be lost on designers and marketing experts. Therefore, make sure the person or people that you chose to work with also have the right technical skills.

Search Engine Optimisation

One of the most important skills the web design team must have is a firm understanding of search engine optimisation (SEO). Having a great website with bad SEO is like building an amazing shop in the middle of nowhere. Sadly, the familiar adage 'if you build it, they will come' does not work with websites. You have to build it in a way that will get your site placed where people can see it. In the English-speaking world, this is all about understanding how Google ranks websites. SEO is a broad topic and entire books have been written on the subject – so I won't attempt to explain everything in one chapter. In summary however, the key factors in SEO at present are the following:

- good, unique content
- good incoming links from relevant and influential sites
- a site that is built in a way that makes it easy for Google to find all the pages.

Again, much like designing a sports car, every single piece of a good website should be carefully crafted to serve a purpose. Every image should be the correct file size (not too big to slow the site down and not too small to degrade the quality); every public facing directory in the site should have a name that accurately reflects what it is; every piece of copy should be carefully checked for spelling and grammar; and each menu should be easy to use and positioned correctly. If you do decide to break with these standard conventions, do it with good reason.

The Basics

Here are some other basics:

1. Your logo should be in the top left hand corner and linked to the home page.

2. Have a good *favicon* (the little icon that shows up in the address bar or on a browser tab). These days, if you don't have a favicon your site looks a bit amateurish. Favicons are also very prominent on some major mobile platforms. By not having a favicon, you are missing a big advertising opportunity and making your site harder to find once it is open on someone's device.

3. Create sensible *title tags* and *meta tags*. This is mainly so your website listing looks good on Google.

4. Put a high quality hosting solution in place. A good place to start is somewhere local to where the majority of your target visitors are based.

5. Use trust symbols. These are things that help verify that a site is trustworthy. This is especially important for smaller companies trading online. An example of a trust symbol would be something like an ISO registration number or an independent customer review. For payment systems, use things like Visa signs or other major trusted symbols. These will help improve your conversion rates and lower your CPA.

30 Worst Website Crimes

And now, here are the 30 worst things you can do to a website without getting arrested (although web designers who perpetrate them should be).

1. 'Lost in space'. Make sure you have a coherent strategy for search engine listings. If your site is hard to find on search engines, far fewer people will visit. Make sure you choose keywords that are specific to your business or organization.

2. A blank or generic title tag. The title tag is vital in achieving high search engine rankings, yet many companies leave these blank or non-specific. They should be descriptive, accurately reflecting the content of the site.

3. Unused meta description tags. These tags show up on Google results and are the doorway to your site. Use them well. A call to action is often the best use of the meta description tag.

4. 'Under construction' pages. If a page isn't ready, then don't put it online.

5. 'Lonely orphans'. Pages that don't have links to them are known as 'orphans' in the trade – and as far as the rest of the world is concerned, they don't exist.

6. 'Alien abduction'. Pages that completely ignore the look and feel of the rest of your website leave users feeling like they've been suddenly transported to a website far, far away.

7. 'Uncharted waters'. Good navigation makes it easy for your users to find stuff. Pages without navigation make it more difficult. If you don't offer them an option, visitors are more likely to close your page than hit the browser's back button.

8. 'The missing link'. Broken links are frustrating for visitors. Use software to check for these – and get them fixed.

9. 'The hidden link'. Links that are hard to find won't get used as often. Make them identifiable by using a contrasting colour, underlining, altering the rollover state etc.

10. 'Jumping jack flash'. Jumping menus are never good – in a restaurant or on a website. Get your web designer to fix them.

11. Typos. Spelling and grammatical mistakes pour cold water over your intended professionalism. Use your spell checker, but don't rely on it blindly either. Spell checkers can be like old dogs – faithful but stupid.

12. Images for text. Text in images can't be read by search engines or screen readers.

13. 'Broken compass'. Once the user learns how to use your site's navigation, keep it the same – don't change it.

14. Lack of contrast. Use contrast, especially between text and background.

15. Random design. Using too many fonts, too many styles, too many weights, too many sizes or too many colours is just too much.

16. Images without the <alt> attribute. That's the little text box that sometimes pops up when your mouse is over an image. Search engines like them and so do your visitors.

17. Improper image format. JPEGs are best for photos and continuous tone images. GIFs are best for images with large areas of flat colour.

18. Poor quality photography. One strong, well-chosen photograph can make any website look great – so what do you think one bad shot will do?

19. Clichéd and overused clip-art.

20. Forced animation. Some people will watch and enjoy your animation. Some people will be in a hurry and want to skip it. Always give them the option.

21. Overly animated animation. Let your animation cycle a few times and then stop it. Also, give the users a 'STOP' button in case they feel dizzy.

22. Blinking text . . . is blinking annoying.

23. No contact address. The purpose of a website is to communicate. Make sure people can find a way to contact you.

24. Reliance on email links. Email links only work if the user has an email program available and correctly configured. And they don't work with Gmail and similar services, so people in libraries or school labs can't use them. Most ISPs offer a form processing script that can convert the contents of a form to an email and send it to you. Use it.

25. "I'll get back to you . . . one day". Ignore spam, of course – but when a legitimate visitor takes the time to contact you, a prompt reply is warranted.

26. Noises off. Unexpected, auto-play sounds are irritating, especially in an office or classroom. Always provide a clear 'OFF' button for sounds.

27. Opening too many windows. Cluttering up someone's screen with a new window every time they click on a link is just plain rude.

28. Cross-browser inconsistencies. Your site should work the same on Mac OS X and Windows: in Safari, Chrome, Firefox and Internet Explorer. Ask your web designer for W3C Compliance.

29. Totally immobile. Your users may not be on a broadband connection. They might be on their BlackBerry. Provide a site that can be used on mobile devices, at least so that they can see your phone number if they are trying to find your office.

30. Out of date, out of mind. Your audience will stop coming back if your site never changes. Either get a CMS (content management system) or make friends with someone who knows HTML.

THE ART OF USER EXPERIENCE DESIGN

by Richard Carman

About Richard Carman

RICHARD CARMAN is the managing director of Pure Innovation, a digital web and mobile application agency that is passionate about technology and developing great code.

A digital expert with a passion for all things web, technology and business related, Richard is mostly either working with technology entrepreneurs to get new web-based ideas off the ground or helping marketing agencies to make the web work for them and their clients in increasingly complex ways.

His first career was as an Army Officer with the Royal Engineers, where he lived by the phrase: "improvise, adapt and overcome" – something which has proved to be an invaluable skill in business. The team he now heads up at Pure Innovation are a very talented bunch who pride themselves on being "a bunch of geeks who like a challenge!"

www.pureinnovation.com | @richardcarman

OUR ABILITY to understand how a piece of software or digital device works is directly proportional to our inclination to use it.

The digital systems that we use everyday are becoming increasingly complex, but they must be intuitive and enjoyable to use or they are simply cast aside in favour of more user-friendly systems. These digital systems include websites, web applications, desktop software, mobile phones, games consoles and the ever increasing spectrum of electronic devices that are now an accepted part of our daily lives.

Any system that requires some form of human-computer interaction (HCI) has a need for user experience (UX) design.

What is UX Design?

UX is all about perception; the emotion a user feels when they interact with a system. "Is this website [for example] easy to use? Do I get value from it? Do I enjoy using it? Do I trust it? Will I return?" These questions run through a user's mind when deciding whether they like an experience enough to delve deeper or to repeat it.

UX design is the art of creating a positive emotional experience that makes a user answer "yes" to all those questions. A UX designer is a person who specialises in that art.

It was Donald Norman, a professor of cognitive science and usability engineering, who originally coined the term "user experience" and brought it into common usage. He was also one of the first people to talk about user-centred design, stating that design decisions should be made on the basis of what users want. Norman wrote the book *The Design of Everyday Things* and co-founded the Nielsen Norman Group with Jacob Nielsen, a professor of HCI considered by many to be a leading web usability consultant. Nielsen continues to write a regular newsletter, *Alertbox* (**useit.com**), on web design matters. Readers who visit that site will not be surprised to learn that Nielsen has also been widely criticised by graphic designers for putting website usability before visual impact.

There is no doubting the fact that users are immediately drawn to eye-catching designs. This is clearly demonstrated by the sheer volume of websites that focus on grabbing our attention with what graphic designers refer to as 'eye candy'. But, as Nielsen argues and experience shows, a beautiful website is not always a good one. Where UX is concerned, beauty is all-too-often just skin deep.

We've all experienced the pain. The page loads for the first time: your immediate emotion is one of pleasure as you are greeted with a graphical masterpiece. Then, bit by bit, your emotion turns to frustration as you struggle to find what you are looking for. You end up going round in circles. And you don't come back.

It simply isn't good enough any more to design websites or other digital experiences that look awesome. We have to focus on a user-centred approach to achieve the best results.

The Key Elements of UX Design

The first and most critical element of UX design is research; if we don't know the 'who, what, why, where and how', then we're just guessing. So before we do anything else it's essential to establish our objectives and user needs:

- What are we trying to achieve?

- What will the user get out of it?

Only when we've successfully answered these questions can we begin to tackle the physical elements.

Let us take a look now at the five key elements that are generally accepted as the building blocks of UX design. In a large organisation there is usually a team working on this process, with individuals or groups responsible for each stage. In this instance, however, we will assume all roles are being fulfilled by a generic UX designer.

Information architecture (IA)

When looking at information architecture for the web, we're interested in the structure of the user interface (UI) and how the end user will find his or her way around the website, using such aids as content channelling, navigation and search. These are the foundations of the UX design process.

Some of the key elements that information architecture addresses are as follows:

- The primary user goals and how they can be achieved by using the website.

- Personas – portraits and profiles of the end users, enabling the UX designer to think like the intended audience.

- Scenarios and user flows – how users move from one piece of content to another under different situations.

- The optimal feature set to engage the user – the optimal approach is the one that channels the user to the desired outcomes, often referred to as goals, as efficiently as possible.

- The search mechanism, including how it works, as well as where it should be placed on the page. Some purist UX designers will claim that adding search functionality to a website is an admittance of their failure to design an intuitive interface. But imagine you are looking for a specific product in a large catalogue and you know the part number: search is most definitely the fastest and most efficient means of finding it. The real power of the digital world is in the ability to filter search results and home in on exactly what we're looking for. The job of the UX designer is to provide the relevant tools to achieve this. And search also has a range of potential options and pitfalls.

- The UI roadmap – often referred to as *user journeys*, which are based on the desired outcomes from a user's visit to your website.

- Global elements – items that are present throughout all site pages, such as primary navigation and footer elements.

- Navigation behaviours and patterns – these are often guesswork at this stage, based on assumptions from the user flows; they will be clarified by user testing in the latter stages.

- Structure diagram or site map – this is the content inventory that gives the UX designer an understanding of the volume of information that has to be organised.

- Information hierarchy – otherwise referred to as the *taxonomy*, the logical cascade of information that will form the navigational structure.

Interaction design (IxD)

The role of interaction design is to build on the information architecture in order to create a rich user experience. At this point the UX designer assumes the responsibility for design concepts or *wireframes*, although these must not be confused with the visual look and feel that comes later. IxD delves into the layout and flow of information and looks at every last element on the page, including:

- Wireframes and prototypes – outline sketches of key screens, enabling a focus on structure and interaction before colour, typography and images can distract. Some popular software tools for wireframing and prototyping include OmniGraffle, Balsamiq, Mockingbird and Mockflow.

- Storyboards – creating a story out of a user journey through a specific process, such as the checkout on an e-commerce website, helps to identify key points of interaction.

- Behaviour of elements – what happens when you drag and drop, mouse over, right click, scroll etc.

IxD is the visualisation of the key information gathered during the information architecture process. It's extremely important to keep it to black and white diagrams at this stage. At the end of the IxD process, everyone involved in the project should have a clear understanding of how the website will function and how key elements will be structured. Colour and images are unwelcome distractions at this stage and only serve to confuse.

Usability

When we get to this stage in the process, it is really important for the UX designer to distance himself from the rest of the processes. Quite simply, you have to think like the end user in order to bring the user experience into context. Once you're in the mindset of the user, you immediately have a different perspective on how easy the website is to use. More importantly, you're able to gain a valuable insight into the emotion that the website is likely to evoke in the user.

Jacob Nielsen refers to the following framework for evaluating usability:

- **Learnability** – how easy it is for users to accomplish basic tasks when they first encounter a design.
- **Efficiency** – how quickly users can perform a task once they've learned the design.
- **Memorability** – how easily users can re-establish proficiency with the design when returning to it after a given period.
- **Errors** – the number of errors a user makes, their severity and the speed of recovery from those errors.
- **Satisfaction** – how pleasant the design is to use.

As soon as the usability element is completed, we're ready to jump into the final design process, armed with valuable insights into what the user is looking for. One of the most important outputs from the usability process is also to identify the key deliverables for usability testing at the end of the project.

Visual design

This is the point at which we finally let the creative guys loose. It's also the point where everyone suddenly has an opinion. That's because brand identities are communicated through the visual design process and therefore create the greatest emotions in the customer. That's why we've left it to the end of the design process. In the early days of web design, the graphic designers leapt in at the very beginning of the UX design process and companies invariably ended up with an awesome design that the client loved but the user hated. Little wonder: it hadn't been created with them in mind.

Some of the key elements that the graphic designers have to consider are:

- **Style guide** – most large organisations have a formal document that dictates how their brand identity should be displayed. In the absence of this, it is up to the graphic designer to create a consistent and complementary style

- **Colour theory** – sympathetic use of colour plays a large part in affecting user emotions, whilst consistent use of a specific colour and style for navigation is a powerful aid to good UX design

- **Typography** – font choices are often dictated by a style guide and corporate brand identity, but this is not always the case. Consideration must be given to scalability for use across multiple platforms, such as desktop, tablet, mobile, etc. You may recall the early limitations of HTML that restricted designers to a small set of web-safe fonts. Well, the advent of webfonts and HTML5 has presented a vast smorgasbord of fonts for the graphic designer to play with. Caution is still advisable, though, to ensure the basics of good design are not cast aside.

- **Information graphics or *infographics*** – facts and figures portrayed in a graphical format to enable the end user to grasp information as quickly as possible

- **Images** – photography and illustrations that visually enhance the communication process.

Functionality

Once all the design elements have been completed, many web designers are guilty of thinking that the UX design process is complete. However, a quick trip back to the beginning of the chapter will remind them that UX is all about the emotions a user feels when using a website. It is therefore important to ensure that the developers and programmers (coders) are part of the UX team, since all the good work above can be undone very quickly if they don't pay attention to the UX.

Some of the key UX elements that the coders have to consider include the following:

- Cross-browser compatibility. One of the biggest challenges for any coder is ensuring that their creation will work across all common browsers. The focus here must be to refer back to the user research we carried out before the UX design process began; you must know what browsers your target audience are likely to be using and code accordingly. It is no good stating 'We don't support IE6' if you're creating an intranet for a corporation that is locked into old software by a dated IT policy and infrastructure.

- Cross-platform compatibility. Equally as challenging are the wide range of platforms and devices that are used to view your website. Again, understanding your target audience will enable you to focus your efforts on the most appropriate platforms. One approach is to develop separate apps for mobile devices. However, a more flexible approach is to use *responsive design*, which allows a coder to create one version of a website that will scale according to the platform being used to view it. A good example of this can be seen at **cssgrid.net**.

- Speed. With broadband internet access becoming the widespread standard, the quickest way to alienate users is to make them wait for a slow website to load. In fact, Google now include speed of access in their ranking algorithm, which in itself should be sufficient incentive for most web developers to speed up their act.

UX Design Concepts and Best Practice

Having looked at the core elements that make up UX design, there are a number of best practice considerations that any good UX designer worth their salt should be concerned with. These include:

Focus on content

I'm sure you've heard the singularly most overused phrase on the internet: "Content is King". Coined by Bill Gates in his 1996 article of the same title, is this still true today? Absolutely, 100%, *yes*. There really can be no denying that good quality content is still the way to your website visitors' hearts. After all, that's why they come, to find good quality information, with Google, Bing, Yahoo and others simply signposting the way.

So what do we mean by good quality content? Is it text, images, sound or video, or a combination of all of these? Well, all have a role to play. Their effectiveness ultimately depends on how they are presented and how easy they are to find.

If your copywriter has done his job properly, he will have identified the kind of content that is important for your target audience; but if he hasn't, you may be left wondering why your bounce rate is so high.

Calls to action and the sales funnel

It's all too easy to become embroiled in the features and benefits of your product or service and forget to point the user at a goal. Every website must have a purpose or goal, regardless or whether it's a business selling products and services or a community for like-minded individuals. Often a website can have multiple goals and it's the job of the UX designer to identify these and ensure that there are clear channels and user journeys that lead to them. We call this the *sales funnel*.

The challenge is to get the user into the sales funnel as quickly and efficiently as possible, and to do this we have to create clear signposts that catch their attention and invite them to follow the white rabbit. We refer to these as *calls to action* (CTA).

CTAs can take a variety of forms, from simple text or buttons stating: "Buy Now", "Add to Basket" or "Contact Us", to more elaborate graphics with a strong message and an invitation to engage.

Testing and measuring

This is arguably the most powerful and important part of any web-design process. Everything we have been through in the UX design process is based on assumptions of what emotions we are likely to evoke in the end user. It's not until we actually test it on a real person that we start to understand whether or not all our theory stacks up.

The challenge we have with testing and measuring the effectiveness of UX design is that traditional quantitative measures are simply inadequate because the information is subjective. It's all about the emotion a user feels. You simply can't put a figure on that.

So we're left with a process that we can't directly measure. What now? The answer is to use the time-honoured approach of trial and error. Some of the techniques that can be used are as follows:

- **A/B or split testing** – also referred to as multivariate testing. This process compares user reactions to two different versions of a user view (usually a web page or email). Many applications now include A/B testing metrics in their standard feature set, enabling you to compare statistics such as traffic volumes, bounce rates and conversion rates for each of the two user views. From the results you can deduce the most effective version for implementation

- **User surveys** – getting back to basics: ask the user what they thought. It's often a good idea to interview a few users first to get a real feel for their emotions. This will enable you to ask the most helpful questions of a larger survey group

- **User-testing** – sitting a group of users in front of your website and asking them to complete specific tasks, whilst you watch and record their actions. Most importantly you must set the task and then watch without offering any input or assistance. This distanced approach is critical to ensure an unbiased view of how they would act in a real world scenario. This is arguably the most powerful and accurate measure of how users will respond to your website. It can be a time-consuming and costly process if done correctly. Consider that you may need to repeat the exercise across a representative range of platforms and browsers to get an accurate picture of how your target audience will react.

The Commercial Case for UX Design

It's all well and good following a process, but if you're building a website for a commercial organisation then you've got one goal in mind, and that's to generate more business. So it's worth considering some of the other factors that really matter to the executive management team in the boardroom.

Regardless of the size of a commercial business, it all boils down to the same things that really matter to the executive team:

Regulatory compliance

As the internet permeates almost every aspect of our daily lives, so the legal implications become more complex and the potential to lose your shirt in the boardroom over a seemingly unnecessary compliance issue is of increasing concern. Therefore, legal and regulatory compliance are much higher up the boardroom agenda these days than ever before.

Some of the key areas to be aware of when working on the UX design process are:

- **Accessibility** and the **Disability Discrimination Act (DDA)** – the UK DDA came into effect in December 1996, and on 1 October 2004 it was updated to require businesses to ensure that their services are fully accessible to disabled people. One implication for your website is that it must be accessible to partially sighted or blind people using screen readers. This is a task for your UX designer.

- **Privacy policies** and the **EU cookie law** – web designers sometimes deposit small snippets of code (cookies) on a user's machine to track their activity. Many of these cookies only last whilst the browser is open, but others stay on the user's machine even when turned off (persistent cookies). On 26 May 2011 a new EU law made it compulsory to obtain a user's consent before storing or retrieving any information on their computer or any other device.

- **Patents, Trademarks and Copyright** – many people wrongly assume that because information is published in the public domain they can simply reuse it as their own. However, patent, trademark and copyright laws do apply on the internet and can be rigorously enforced by some organisations

- **Security** and the **Information Commissioner's Office (ICO)** – quite simply, if you are storing information about a user on your website, then you have a legal obligation to protect the security of that data.

Market share

Most businesses are not unique. They have competitors vying for a share of the same market. Anything that offers a competitive advantage is going to awaken the interest of the executive team and good UX design processes can offer a significant nudge in the right direction.

Return on investment (ROI)

The single most important factor that's likely to galvanise a positive response from the executive management team is the prospect of adding a percentage to the bottom line. The UX design process can be a lengthy and costly one, so it is critical to demonstrate its ability to create more benefit than cost, or in boardroom parlance a good 'ROI'.

ONLINE REPUTATION

by Alexia Leachman

About Alexia Leachman

ALEXIA LEACHMAN is a Brand Strategist and Head Trash Clearance Specialist. She helps people and businesses to find their mojo by helping them to tap into and build their brands. This usually involves helping them to tell their story, raise their profile, build their digital presence and manage their reputation as well as some good old head trash clearance. She has worked with staff from the BBC, Estée Lauder, Experian, and Skype and her private clients have included a reality TV star and her beauty brand, multi award- winning photographer, a bestselling author and a Dragon from Dragons' Den.

Alexia is also the founder of **HeadTrash.co.uk**, the home of the most powerful head trash clearance techniques in the world. Her mission to clear the world of its head trash is done through one-to-one sessions and events, and running training courses for those who want to learn how to do the same.

Alexia is a regular contributor to **Freshbusinessthinking.com** and is the resident Personal Branding Expert for **BusinessMindedModel.com**. She has contributed to the book Mash-Up by Ian Sanders and David Sloly and is a regular commentator in women's magazines and on BBC radio.

You can find out more at **www.blossomingbrands.com** and **www.headtrash.co.uk** and you can follow her on Twitter @AlexiaL and @head_trash

WHEN IT COMES to marketing, we know the internet is no longer optional but essential, and companies are increasingly diverting their spend away from traditional channels such as press and TV to the online space. Interestingly, though, some of the more peripheral marketing activities of the web, such as the use of social media, have not been integrated into the marketing mix as quickly as other activities such as display ads and video.

Company and brand marketers were slow to grasp the potential of social media and similar online tools, an oversight they have since tried to redress. Those who were quick to recognise the opportunities were individuals: people like you and me; regular Joes, freelancers and business owners. People *without* huge marketing budgets.

And when you have virtually no budget to tell the world that you're here, it forces you to become creative. People had to invest time rather than money to get it right. Understanding how to use Twitter effectively in the early days was not the easiest of tasks; so many passed it by. The cash-poor, time-rich freelancers and business owners who invested time in getting to grips with it, and similar tools like Facebook and LinkedIn, prospered.

But the cash-rich, time-poor busy marketers by and large stuck with the old ways, in company climates that probably prohibited the use of social networking sites anyway.

When they eventually came to play catch-up, they found the rules of the game had changed. Fundamentally, what happened can be summarised as a shift towards what we might call a *brand conversation*. Engaging with your customers and fans so intimately had not really been possible before; it required a new approach.

Values such as transparency and authenticity have become all-important. Customers want to have 'real' conversations and not feel as though they are being sold to. There has been – and in some places, there still is – an awkward transition from a broadcast mentality to one where brands let their customers create the message with them.

> **WHAT NOT TO DO**
> Check out 14 of the worst social media mistakes made by big companies, including getting drunk at Red Cross, tweeting about shooting elephants, and fake blogs about hair: **tinyurl.com/8jhecv4**

Reputations live or die online. This is the marketing environment in which we must operate. The rest of this chapter will explore how we go about building a reputation online.

Reputation is What You Make it

Your reputation is based on what you say and what you do. This is true of individuals and of companies. It's the accumulation of responses to this that forms your reputation. So, if you have a questionable reputation, the first place to look is in the mirror. In other words, in building a reputation online, you first need to ensure that you have a good reputation in the real world.

The same goes if you have *no* reputation. If you're trying to change your reputation in any way – to create one or change one – the place to start is with yourself. And this is where we need to start before we can engage in an effective brand conversation online.

Who (or what) are you?

A huge part of what you're going to be doing is showing how you add value. This applies whether you're building your personal or business brand. But it becomes a difficult task if you're not really sure what makes your business awesome, or why people should choose you over someone else in the first place.

So before you begin any reputation-building activities on the web, you need to be crystal clear on a few things.

What you do

While what you do might seem a little too obvious, the point here is the importance of finding a way of articulating it that is clear and memorable and makes you seem indispensable.

The relentless march of technology is transforming the way we communicate, work and play. The upside to this is that there are infinite new ways for companies and people to make money. The downside is that we don't always understand exactly how that money is made. With everything changing so quickly, it can be difficult to ensure that other people understand exactly what it is that you actually do. If they aren't clear, they are less likely to talk about you, and it's the conversations that people have about you (or your business or brand) that help you build your brand.

On the other hand, you might be doing something very simple and easy to understand, but there are lots of other people or companies doing exactly the same thing. The trick here is to find a way to articulate what you do in a way that makes you to stand out. This is an opportunity for you to be creative with language. Combine words that might not normally be seen together. Avoid descriptions that could be mistaken for a rival's. Don't be afraid to be radically different.

Being remembered ⤳ being referred or recommended = reputation

What you stand for

Your values are communicated in everything you do. Actions speak louder than words; online, they can scream. A strong brand is built when you consistently reinforce your values through your actions. Clarify them in advance. Never forget them. Check any online action against them before you go through with it.

Your strengths

Great businesses and brands (personal and business) are built on strengths. Take time to uncover your strengths and what makes you awesome. This is why people like, respect and choose you.

Who you are talking to

This is a nicer way of referring to your *target market* or your *target audience*. There's a good reason for it; as we're in the online space, it's about the *conversation*. So, who are you talking to? Who are the people that you help? Who are the people that you're trying to influence?

For a business, these will be stakeholders; customers, shareholders, relevant press and bloggers, employees . . . For an individual, this will depend on personal goals and aspirations. A business owner will probably want to ensure that she has visibility with her target customers, employees, competitors, investors and her peer group.

So answering this question is key. You only have finite resources. You don't want to waste your them talking to everyone in the hope that *someone* will be interested. You also want to be able to get the tone and focus of your conversation right; knowing your audience is vital for that.

Your story

Using storytelling to deliver the answers to these questions can be a great help. Stories engage on an emotional level, and most people buy emotionally (despite thinking that they buy rationally!).

If you can build a compelling story around who you are and what you offer, you increase the likelihood of standing out. Great stories travel well. They can do wonders for your reputation.

And they often have that viral quality which leads to "Aaah yes, I've heard of you!" when you introduce yourself.

* * *

Once you've covered your basics, you're ready to move onto the more practical aspects of building a reputation online. As in the real world, there are a few important digital touch points in building a brand. Brand touch points are those areas where your audience comes in contact with what you do. They are where you have the opportunity to make an impression.

In the online world, two important touch points I'd like to focus on are:

- what you say about yourself on your 'about' page
- your online identity.

It's All About the 'About'

Did you know that the *about page* on a website is always one of the most read pages? A wonderfully crafted about page which includes a compelling and engaging narrative will do wonders in persuading people to buy into you.

To help you to get it right you need to work from this assumption: people are nosey. They want to know everything about you (or the people behind the business). They want to know the *real* you, not the business you. And they want pictures.

Of course, you need to mention some of the serious stuff that gives you credibility; but it's not qualifications and fancy titles that will get people onside. It's being human.

Business about pages

If you are a business, do not use the about page to expand further on the ins and outs of your service or product propositions. That kind of information needs to be elsewhere. This page is your opportunity to get people to *fall in love* with your business, and people can only fall in love with emotional and human content.

Some of the things to communicate on a business about page can include:

- Why the business was started. Who started it. The history of the business.
- The values you try to bring to what you do.

Detail and interesting examples are key. For me, the most important thing is to shout about the people behind the business. In every business, one of your greatest assets is your people – tell the world about them. They are also the one asset you have that is always unique. So they must be key to what differentiates you from your competitors.

Here are some questions to answer when putting together content about them:

- Who are the people behind the business now? (Names, background, personalities.)

- Why are they involved in the business – what gets them out of bed in the morning?

- What do they bring to the business? What do they do for the business?

- What do they look like? Photos please!

Personal about pages

If it's your personal website, try to avoid boring people with lists of qualifications and fancy job titles. Instead, tell people *who* you are; *why* you're doing what you do; *what* you love about it.

Open up. Try to be comfortable talking about the whole you, not just the 'work' you. Include some life challenges that you've overcome, or embarrassing failures. These things show your human side. Everyone can relate to difficulties – who's not faced them?

By exposing the whole you, you're offering people ways of connecting to you, maybe through common experience. It might be one of these tiny details that actually swings it for you. In a world littered with qualifications and titles, the best way to stand out is by sharing the personal stuff.

And don't forget to include a great photo!

Your Digital Identity

To build your reputation online you need to make it as easy as possible to be found. Of course, there are the usual SEO tricks that you need to be aware of, but what I'm talking about here is your digital identity.

Given the numerous social media platforms that you can participate in, you need to make it as easy as possible for people who are connected to you in one network to find you in others. If some of your Twitter followers decide to search for you on Instagram or Pinterest, it'll be much easier for them if you use the same username and avatar. That way they know they've found the right person.

And mistakes can happen if things aren't obvious. Sometimes customers start following a similarly named account by mistake. When the account doesn't respond to a question or a complaint, the problem can soon bubble over and damage your reputation.

Finding yourself

For many people, finding the right digital ID to express their business can be an utter headache, especially if they've a common or ambiguous name. These questions can help guide a brainstorm:

- What do you want to be known for? What are your areas of expertise? And what about your style of working? What's your philosophy and approach?

- What is your current digital presence? What networks are you present in? What blogs or online profiles have you got?

- What happens when people Google your name? Are the results indicative of what you're trying to achieve? Do they enhance your prospects of making connections or sales? Or do any of these results detract or confuse?

The right digital identity will double-down on your strengths, cut against your weaknesses, and above all be clear and consistent.

What Are You Doing?

With clear reputational objectives and an effective identity in place, it's time to start engaging in the brand conversation. Ultimately, this all boils down to two core activities:

- taking part in what's going on
- sharing content.

Note how this is a significant shift from the old marketing model of:

- interrupting what's going on
- telling people why they should like you.

A brand conversation is not about selling. Nor is it about making sure everyone looks at you. It's simply about drawing alongside customers and potential customers and helping them; being in the conversation as a useful participant not an ad-spouting zombie.

Are you engaging?

Sociability is something I mentioned in the introduction to this chapter. Conversations are not a one-way affair. The clue is in the name *social media*. It's all about being social! And that means having social skills: the ability to engage and converse, be nice to people, show respect for others.

The lack of these is magnified in the online space. Being rude, boring or self-important will attract a similar result online as it would in-person. The bad news it that word of it can spread far more quickly and permanently. The good news is that anyone can be an effective engager if they want to be.

It all boils down to:

- **Getting stuck in!** An obvious one, but many people prefer lurking. They listen, read and watch, but they don't take part. If you don't take part, your online presence is not really a presence at all, let alone one capable of bearing or developing a reputation.

- **Responding in a timely manner** to all communication from others, especially if they're followers or fans.

- **Not being negative or rude**, even in response to negativity or rudeness. Whatever goes online, stays online – a slip of the tongue, even an excusable one, will be there forever for all to see.

- **Trying to avoid just posting your own content.** This is dangerously close to the one-way approach of the old days, and hints of self-importance. So link to, and talk about, others. Promotional messages need to be kept to an absolute minimum: always less than 30% of your total content.

Sharing content

Deciding what content to publish and share can be what gives you your online reputation in the first place. If you have a well-written blog and are first to share breaking news in your sector, this can help establish you as an expert. What people will be buying into is your ability to filter the information that comes your way and to share items that mean something to someone who has the same interests.

Note the word *filtering*. What this doesn't mean is that you share everything that you read, everything that you do and everything that you think. Creating digital noise for others will only encourage them to ignore you.

It all comes down to trust

What underpins everything we've looked at in this chapter is *trust*.

Can you be trusted?

In taking the time to build a strong online reputation, all of your goals can be summed up as trying to establish trust with your audience.

- You need to be clear about who you are and how you can help others.

- You need to be easy to find and easy to get along with.

- You need to cherish your audience and reward them with valuable content rather than self-promotion.

Trust and reputation are intrinsically linked. Together, they are the currency of the new information economy; one in which you and your business can prosper if you jump into the brand conversation with your eyes open. Hopefully this chapter has helped you to do that.

LOCAL INTERNET MARKETING

by Andrew Rayner

About Andrew Rayner

ANDREW RAYNER is a self-professed search marketing geek with a passion for extracting knowledge from data.

Having studied Information Systems at the University of Surrey he went on to work in IT in analytical roles. His ability to learn and keen interest in commercial knowledge saw him rapidly advanced from a junior support role to IT Manager in just two years. However, he realised that life as an employee was not for him when an entrepreneurial opportunity came along in the form of an offer to co-found a technology business and after six years helping other small businesses to take advantage of technology the .com boom led him to starting his own business.

As MD and search marketing strategist at **e-mphasis.com** he established a niche in local internet marketing methods, culminating in the company being a finalist in the National Business Awards for Excellence in Marketing in 2010. Andrew continues to work with businesses of all sizes, both in the UK and internationally and provides innovative marketing solutions, advice and regularly speaks on internet marketing topics.

Shrewd local businesses (or branches of larger retailer chains) are beginning to realise that the return on investment (ROI) of internet marketing to a local targeted audience is much greater than that achieved marketing nationally or globally. This is opening up new opportunities in internet marketing well suited to businesses that can only service a limited area cost-effectively, or those that rely on the consumer trying the product or visiting their premises – pubs, restaurants, designer clothing etc.

How Does Local Internet Marketing Work?

Each of the familiar forms of internet marketing has an equivalent local internet marketing cousin. Below are the most important forms, highlighting some of the benefits of the local element in the marketing mix.

Local email marketing

Major brands have traditionally focused on blanket email marketing to consumers, or at best restricting mailing content to specified consumer interests. But by linking email marketing with relevant aspects of *location* instead, businesses can increase trust and engagement. They can:

- invite consumers to local events, assured of far higher take-up
- tie in offers to local activities such as market days, festivals, etc.
- use email as part of attracting customers through local celebrities, social groups (both off and online) and bundle deals with relevant local businesses.

Local pay-per-click marketing

Google's AdWords (**adwords.google.co.uk**) and AdWords Express (**www.google.co.uk/adwords/express**) offer businesses location-based targeting. However, searches *from* a given location as well as those that include reference to a location can be relevant. This is referred to as near (my location) and far (the location I have referenced) targeting.

Local social media marketing

Connecting with local influencers on social media provides an ideal way to boost your business locally. Identifying these people can actually be quite straightforward. Start by searching for your location on major social networks, and then use profile information to narrow it down. Monitoring and evaluation tools such as Klout (**www.klout.com**) and Empire Avenue (**www.empireavenue.com**) can also provide insights into someone's level of influence related to location.

Identify and build a rapport with relevant local communities and celebrities. But be careful who you align yourself to. As with any association, it can have a negative as well as positive result. Above all, ensure that it will look right for your target consumer.

Local online advertising

You can also advertise your business to local community groups, press, blog and news sites. This is often strangely overlooked, but it's a great opportunity to reach both a target area and a specific consumer demographic.

It's also worth considering if your site could profit from linking with other local businesses online, or hosting their adverts on your pages.

Local search engine optimisation (SEO)

This is, in my experience, the worst implemented of the various kinds of local online marketing. But it's never been more important. Google is now beginning to integrate local results not only into web searches but also into shopping searches and social media activity.

An effective local search marketing strategy goes far beyond having a presence on search engine business listings. You also need to understand relevant local search terms for your business and build them into your website content. Often with SEO, people focus on the product or service that the business offers and completely miss the opportunity to leverage location. It is generally the case with SEO that the more specific the phrase you target, the less competition and the higher search result position you are likely to achieve. Adding location to your target search phrases can often pay rapid dividends.

However, if your business is relevant to people far and wide, you may need to be positioned to appear local to them as well. Using multiple location-focused pages on your website that have been optimised for search can help achieve this.

Given the importance of local SEO, the rest of this chapter will explore how any business can get on top of it profitably.

Local Search Marketing – The Basics

There are a number of simple techniques often used by mass market agencies and espoused by former offline business directories, such as *BT for Business* and *Yell*, to help businesses get started with a local presence online. Although not all-sufficient, they are a good place to start when it comes to local SEO.

Best of all, these are techniques that almost any dynamic business can make use of itself without getting tied up in marketing contracts.

Use a local domain

Consider purchasing a domain for your website that includes your business name (or type) *and* location. For example, *www.readingbikeshop.co.uk*. It may not be terrifically pretty, but it works in conjunction with other aspects of search marketing.

Page URLs (web page addresses)

Using page names that reflect key product or industry phrases like *www.mydomain.com/bicycle-repairs-rg1* can be a useful way to draw in other relevant searches.

Google business listing

Go to **maps.google.co.uk** and search for your business. If you're not listed, go to **places.google.com** and add your business. Even if you are listed, make sure that you claim your entry (something you may need expert advice on depending on your technical knowledge). Check the quality of any reviews already attached to your listing. You may need to alert Google to any unreasonably negative or abusive comments that you've received.

Links to your website

If you get the opportunity to have your site linked to from another site, make sure (if possible) that you include reference to location as well as the business name or type in the text of the link. Links don't *have* to point at your homepage! Think about which page of your site is the most relevant for the source and topic of the link, especially if it relates to a specific location.

Create a local 'landing page'

Consider creating a page (or pages) on your website specifically targeting local consumers. Use the leverage that your location provides in helping people trust you over the competition. Talk about what your business gives back to the community and reference any influential customers (subject to their approval!).

Name, address, telephone number

Make sure that every mention of your company includes your business name, address and telephone number exactly as it is presented in the real world.

In order to achieve this you may need to conduct an audit. Businesses get referenced on a variety of websites over their lifetime. Often that means there may be out of date, incomplete or simply incorrect details floating around on the web. This depresses visibility in search results. Usual culprits include business directories, communities, industry associations and articles in the press.

Hard-searching for two items of the address (i.e. putting the terms in "quote marks") should help you find instances of this.

Newer businesses may also find spurious details of former premises or phone number owners.

As you undertake this 'audit', make a note of all the sites that list your business, even those that do so correctly. You'll want to correct the mistaken ones, but both they and the correct ones will play an equal part in SEO work later on.

Finally, don't forget to check the maps listings on search engines.

As an aside it can also be quite an enlightening exercise to conduct this same process for key competitors. This may help you to identify opportunities to list your business that you may have overlooked.

Research Your Local Search Battlefield

There are probably a number of search terms relevant to your business products and services. Now it's time to think about how they might be searched for in the context of location.

Tools such as Google's Keyword Tool (**adwords.google.com /o/keywordtool**) will tell you what the most searched-for phrases are for your industry, product or services. That's all well and good for global or national SEO. But the best kind of SEO also draws on lateral thinking and extra searching to pick out the long tail of search terms, and that's something even more relevant to local SEO.

- You can also research the most searched-for phrases that include your town, village and first part of your business' postcode to see if any of these phrases are relevant to your business. If they are, use them.

- Ask family, friends or neighbours what they might search for to find a local business that sells what yours does.

- Maintain a list of these and ensure that, if your business offering changes, you make changes to your local SEO.

Having identified the most relevant and searched-for phrases, you need to find out whether you have any chance of achieving a decent result position in searches for these phrases. This means assessing the quality of your competition's SEO. Again, without some search marketing knowledge this can be very complex. Start by performing a search for the phrase you have identified as ideal e.g. 'Bicycle shop in Reading' and see which search results already appear on the first page of the search engine. These could include:

- pages of your own website (hopefully)

- pages of competitors' websites

- local business listings

- image or video results

- local directory or business association results

- social networking profiles and pages

- review sites.

If you are familiar with SEO terminology such as 'page rank', 'inbound links' and 'meta tags', these are a good starting place to assess the quality of any competitor results.

For those less knowledgeable, use a systematic approach to placing or requesting links from any non-competitive website or ask an expert for help.

Don't Just Appear in Search, Dominate It!

Imagine the effect on a consumer searching for a particular product or service in a local area to find that every single search result on the first page of the search engine for the phrase they have typed relates to the same business.

Many marketing agencies work to achieve a top-of-page result for their clients. Real success, though, is to fill the entire first page. Now this may seem impossible. But we're not looking to make our site the only one that appears in these results (which would indeed be impossible), but to make sure that directory sites, social media profiles and review sites featuring content about us come next. It is entirely possible, with a bit of effort and knowhow, to achieve this.

The good news is that many of the pages you're interested in appearing on – those directories, profiles, hubs etc. – will be on the first page already for local searches. Assess those pages to find out how you can position yourself prominently on them.

One of the added benefits of having several of the top ten search results referencing your business is that you will have a reduced risk of being affected by changes to the search 'algorithm' (the mathematical function maintained by the search engines to decide in which order search results should be presented).

Local Internet Marketing Doesn't Stop

Like most internet marketing, simply going through the process once isn't enough. Search marketing in particular requires continued effort. Analysing the impact of your local search marketing on an ongoing basis is critical.

But it is not enough to simply head to a search engine, type in a phrase you want to appear under, and see where your site ranks. Google has been tailoring search results to individual users based on their search and browsing history for some time. So have all search engines (with the exception of **www.duckduckgo.com**). This means that the results you see are different to those other consumers will get.

So Google analytics (**www.google.com/analytics**) and webmaster tools are invaluable for finding out how you are really getting on.

These tools will provide key performance indicators such as the number of impressions (or appearances) of your pages in searches, the number of website (and page) visitors you receive, and even the number of successful visits (assuming you have a target page e.g. transaction confirmation).

What you can measure you can improve

From this data you can work out the effectiveness of your local sales funnel and the conversion factors at each stage. You might have, for example:

- 1,000 impressions (appearances in search)
- 80 visits to the website = 8%
- 4 sales = 5% of visitors, 0.4% of impressions

Using data such as this you can monitor your marketing against your high level business goals. By drilling down in to the details you can also see whether individual phrases in searches or those containing certain words (or locations) are more or less likely to contribute sales to this total and therefore whether you should adapt the focus of your search marketing.

Convenience and trust will always be factors that people value when choosing where to shop. Location is a factor in both. Any business can take advantage of local internet marketing, whatever their product or service and no matter how big or small they are. Even global marketing can be considered the sum of many locales; and with the increase in mobile internet usage, local web marketing will only be of increasing importance.